JOURNEY WITHOUT A MAP

JOURNEY WITHOUT A MAP

Growing Up Italian: A Memoir

DONNA CARUSO

thistledown press

Library and Archives Canada Cataloguing in Publication
Caruso, Donna
Journey without a map : growing up Italian : a memoir / Donna Caruso.

ISBN 978-1-897235-36-2

1. Caruso, Donna. 2. Caruso, Donna—Family. 3. Italian
Canadians—Biography. 4. Italian Americans—New Jersey—Biography.
5. Motion picture producers and directors—Canada—Biography. 6. Authors,
Canadian (English)—20th century—Biography. I. Title.
PS8555.A7736Z47 2008   791.4302′3092   C2008-900079-X

Cover photograph
Cover and book design by Jackie Forrie
Printed and bound in Canada

Thistledown Press Ltd.
633 Main Street
Saskatoon, Saskatchewan, S7H 0J8
www.thistledownpress.com

 Canada Council   Conseil des Arts
for the Arts   du Canada

 Canadian   Patrimoine
Heritage   canadien

We acknowledge the support of the Canada Council for the Arts, the Saskatchewan Arts Board, and the Government of Canada through the Book Publishing Industry Development Program for our publishing program.

ACKNOWLEDGEMENTS

Thanks to Dave Margoshes and Harriet Richards for their editing expertise, and thanks to CBC Radio for broadcasting so many of my stories and plays over the past twenty years. Special thanks to the Saskatchewan Writers Guild for their constancy and encouragement, and to Thistledown Press.

Very special thanks to my family, everywhere, those here and those who have passed on, for embracing me as one of their own, and for creating these and all our stories.

With love to my grandchildren, Erica, Ada Grace, and Niccolo

CONTENTS

THE CLOTHESLINE

OUR FATHER

MOTHER MARY

THE CLOTHESLINE

Italian Christmas

Christmas for Italians, for the people so close to the Pope they could be Santa Claus and jump down his Vatican chimney with presents, Christmas for all my Italian relatives tending sheep on the hillsides in Italy, for all my relatives with stables and donkeys, with ox tail soup for supper, Christmas for us brings us to table together, to look skyward together at the singing stars, because at Christmas Italians are happy with their Bambino God who loves his mother and who comes to visit from far away and stays for a good long time. Italians love that kind of God. Not an angry God, not a mighty God, not a know-it-all God, but an infant son with a family and a tableful of relatives and neighbours.

Letter To Louie About Cooking Pasta

Louie, I love the idea of teaching you how to cook pasta. It really makes me feel like an ancestor. When I was young, so many times I stood by the stove watching my mother cook pasta, and now I'm teaching you. It's moments like these that make me weep for joy.

I will not teach you how to make your own noodles from scratch, Louie, because the only time I ever did it myself, I and everybody else lived to regret it. So now you know that even your mother has limitations. And there's no Santa Claus, either. Life goes on.

So, first of all, make sure you buy the best quality pasta available. Nothing that will stick together when cooked, like the noodle art you made in grade one. That was then, Louie, this is now. Put aside the things of a child and get some grown-up pasta. Pasta from Italy is the best, very, very, high quality, which only makes sense because Italians are the pasta people. I know they say the Chinese invented spaghetti, but we are the pasta artists. The Italians were the ones to bring form and beauty to the pasta world — Ziti, Tortellini, Rotelli, Vermicelli, Gnocchi, Farfalle, to name a few. Each type has its own unique shape and so, a different texture to hold the sauce and tantalize the tongue. You decide which kind you think will make your tongue happiest and buy those.

Now you'll need a huge pot. A huge pot is one you could stick your whole head in right up to the neck. Don't be shy; if you're in doubt, measure. The best pots are the white enamel ones made in Poland — we make the pasta, they make the pots, that's good international relations. But there are lots of different kinds of pots. Someday, after I'm gone, you'll have my macaroni pot to remember me by, with the wisdom of all those years of cooking pasta. The tales it could tell! But until then, you'll need your own, so get a great big one with a nice heavy bottom. Sounds like I'm giving you advice about a wife. I could give you some help there, too, but you're too young for that. But not too young for pasta!

You have to fill the pot almost all the way up with water. Add a few tablespoons of salt to the water, and some red wine vinegar if you're using an aluminum pot. The vinegar is to keep the aluminum from turning black — that's chemistry, you know, just like at school in the lab. Then you put the pot of water on the stove over high heat until it boils. In case you didn't know, Louie, water boiling looks like Uncle Nick dancing at a wedding.

Now prepare yourself, because it will take quite a while for the water to boil. Always, always, you must be prepared to have patience in the kitchen. They say a watched pot never boils. Well, it's that way with most things in life. The more you want something to happen, the slower it is in happening. But if you busy yourself with other things while you're waiting, in no time there it is like nobody's business. So while you're waiting for the water to boil, work around the kitchen, or just sit down and think for a while. Thinking is allowed, Louie. Some of the most famous people thought about things, some full time.

When the water is boiling, you put in the pasta and stir it up once with a wooden spoon. It will take 8-10 minutes to cook the pasta, and you must stay right there in front of the stove all that time. Pasta is very touchy and it knows when it is being neglected, so stay put.

Once the pasta is in the pot, lower the heat to medium-high; you want the water to be hot enough to cook the pasta quickly, but not so hot that the pasta will stick to the bottom of the pot. This is where you have to be sensitive, Louie. A sensitive person knows how their pasta is doing. They say nowadays that women like sensitive men. You know why? Because they cook good pasta, that's why.

Every couple of minutes stir the pasta up from the bottom, so nothing sticks. But don't stir too much or the pasta will be gummy. I don't know why it gets gummy, but it does. Pasta's funny that way.

When you first put the pasta in they are stiff, but as they cook, they relax, like they're enjoying a nice hot bath. Their colour changes a little, too, so that you can sort of see through them. When you notice this, it's time to taste the pasta to see if they're done. I'll tell you right now, Louie, that tasting the pasta is the only sure way to tell if they're done. Once I heard a lady on the radio saying that to tell if pasta is done, you throw it against the wall. If it sticks, it's done. This is crazy, Louie. Can you imagine what the lady's wall looks like? It'd be worse than having a dog. So, you taste.

In the final seconds of cooking, your pasta can change dramatically, as much as Aunt Josie after a glass of wine. So, as soon as your pasta tastes done, you have to hurry up. Louie, this is a big moment. Bring your pasta to the sink and strain it through a colander. Then give the colander a few brisk shakes to get rid of any lingering drops of water. The steam will rise and you'll recognize the pasta's starchy-sweet smell, familiar because you grew up following me around our nice Italian kitchen.

Okay then Louie, put your pasta into a big bowl and ladle a little tomato sauce onto it so it doesn't stick, and mix it up a bit, but not too much. Whatever you do, don't leave your pasta sitting in water and don't run cold water over your pasta after you've strained it. These mistakes make a perfectly good pasta go bad. It's a shame.

Now serve yourself some pasta with tomato sauce and parmagiana cheese on top and enjoy!

Bon Appetito!

Love and kisses,

Mom

The Cup

My grandmother's crystal wine glasses
Everything tastes better in them
they chant her prayers and hold the sparkle of her smile
reflect the glow of her candles lit, beseeching Heaven's favour
As you hold her glass
the warm lips of my family still sip at the rim
celebrating Baptisms, Confirmations, Communions
and every Sunday, birthday, anniversary,
and every graduation from high school
Celebrating with water and wine
the crystal resonating the happiness
the laughter
the caring of the cooks
the sweetness of that time
of bread broken
of lives classical in pattern
of faces familiar and familiar and familiar
family
See? The DNA we know so well today
lies in trace amounts on crystal stem and rim
where even science can see who drank this cup
and in half-life tell the time of contact
whose hand, whose lips,

stained glass
The olive-skinned who called each by name
and remembered
palms open to Heaven
a fingerprint in ash pressed against the forehead
eyes closed when seeing God, or the dearly departed
each would remember the sharing of food and drink forever
and offer it for us all
Do this in remembrance of me, said Jesus, and Grandma, and
Aunt Josie, and Uncle Nick, and all the rest
Take this cup and share it
This is the cup of my bloodline
My grandmother's crystal glasses welcome the wine I pour for
you
Wine and water
Blessed be the memory
Blood and wine and water

Drink
Lift up your hearts
Drink
Take this all of you and you and you and
Drink
Each glass a prayer for us

THE CLOTHESLINE

THE CLOTHESLINE'S SOCKS, SHIRTS, AND BED SHEETS
stretch across the summer prairie, across time and space, across
generations, the prairie wind breathing memories alive again —
people long gone, journeys of long ago — lifted against the
endless blue sky; the clothesline a poor man's drive-in screen,
playing an ocean of dreams and stories.

I've lived on the Saskatchewan prairie for more than thirty
years. When people ask me how I got here, I tell them there's a
lot to be learned from laundry. Until 1929 all my relatives did
their laundry in Italy. I asked my mother about growing up in
Conca a la Compagna, her village on a mountaintop south of
Naples, and she described the river that ran along the lower part
of their village. They would beat the clothes against the rocks
in a place where the water swirled and rushed. They'd scrub the
clothes with their homemade soap, and suck on them to see if
the soap was rinsed out. If the soap taste was gone, the clothes
were clean.

They didn't use clotheslines in Conca. They threw their
clothes over bushes, they threw them over the grasses so that
the sun could use the chlorophyll in the green leaves to bleach
the white to a brighter white.

Because all the clothes were white.

They were all made out of sheep's wool. My mother was a shepherdess. She'd spend her days walking on the hillsides with her sheep, under the olive trees, singing and enjoying the sunshine. Olive trees are short, my mother is short, the sheep are short. I think that's why Italians are short — because they spend so much time walking under the olive trees, all the tall Italians in the gene pool long ago eliminated by low-lying branches.

When my mother was a girl, they made all their own clothes. They made every piece of fabric they used. Absolutely everything — blouses, sheets, tablecloths, dish towels — everything. They would bring the sheep in from the hills for shearing, and then take the shorn wool to begin making cloth. The girls would twist the wool fibers delicately between their fingertips to make it into thread. My mother felt proud that her hands were perfect for this — long thin fingers, strong fingers. She was better than any of her sisters in this work, better at twisting the fibers into threads. Her mother would use a loom to spin the fibers into white clothes for everyone in the family. All the clothes started out white, made out of sheep's wool. Some clothes, like the skirts and pants for the adults, were dyed a dark colour, but the children's clothes, bed sheets, and tablecloths always stayed as white as the sheep they came from.

I asked my mother the most basic questions because the details of her life in Italy always surprised me. I had asked her what they slept on, did they have mattresses, and she smiled, transported to a different time and space. Yes, she said, they had something like mattresses, big pillow cases stuffed with sheep wool, and every morning they would take a wooden rake with a handle as long as my mother was tall and reach in to fluff up the wool so the beds would be comfortable again for another night's sleep. The sheep might as well have borne the family name they were so much a part of the household.

River cloth, sheepskin, sheepskin, sheepskin . . .

If I were going to make a clothesline for my family's story, I'd start with a blue cloth for the river where they washed their clothes. And I'd add right next to it a sheepskin, maybe two or three, because the sheep were part of everything in Italy. And next I'd add a bed sheet. There's one on every clothesline everywhere in the entire world because sleep is part of life, just as night is part of every day, and our dreams spin the clotheslines of our minds and hearts.

River cloth, sheepskin, sheepskin, sheepskin, bed sheet . . .

Whenever I see sheets billowing on a clothesline, I think of my grandparents, my mother's mother and father. My mother's mother, Michelina, was from the wealthiest family in the tiny village of Conca a la Compagna. They had the biggest house, they had the most influence, her father was the most important man in the village.

Michelina fell in love with Vincenzo, my grandfather, whose family was the poorest in the village, a family that was so poor they didn't have any house at all. When I went to Italy with my parents in 1989, we were driving up the mountain to the top where Conca a la Compagna looked out over the countryside, and as we were going up and up and up, suddenly my mother stretched out her arm and pointed to a cave in the mountainside just below the village and she blurted out, "That's where your grandfather lived." He was born in a cave. Lived in a cave.

And my grandmother, Michelina, fell in love with this caveman.

Her father was furious when he learned they wanted to get married. He said, "It's impossible! It's like the slipper marrying the boot; it will never work!" But my grandmother convinced him. I think she did that by getting pregnant — it used to work in those days. And so, my mother's mother and father were married.

But in an Italian village, everyone knows who you are and who your family was fifty generations ago. Everyone knew my grandmother had married beneath her. Everyone knew my grandfather, Vincenzo, didn't deserve a wife such as Michelina. And no matter what he did, no matter how much time passed, he would never be worthy of Michelina in their eyes.

After their first son, Alberto, was born, Vincenzo said to Michelina, "We should go to America." My grandmother thought he had lost his mind. Why would they leave all the land she had in Italy, why would they go to such a far away and so strange a place as America? My grandfather told her why. It was because in America, everybody could make it big; it didn't matter what you used to be or who your family was in Italy; in America, everyone could become a somebody.

My grandmother wasn't impressed. She already was somebody in Conca. Why should she give up everything and go to America where she was a nobody so that she could be a somebody again sometime in the future? My grandfather tried to make her understand. My grandmother tried to make *him* understand. Nobody was understanding anything. My grandmother said to her foolish husband, "You want to go to America, go. But I will stay here with Alberto. You go. Go. Go be somebody." My grandfather, confident that he could be somebody in America and that he could make Michelina and the whole village proud of him, left my grandmother and their infant son, Alberto, and sailed to America.

I think of him when I see a bed sheet on a clothesline billowing up against the sky like the sail on a sailing ship. I think of my grandfather crossing that enormous ocean, his dreams filling his head like the wind fills sails. I think of the journeys of all the immigrants. Of the sails of a thousand journeys since the beginning of time. Of the ancient winds that blew across the oceans like the breath of dreams, of sighs, like the breath of those left behind on the shores. Like the breaths we breathe now, in and out, the breaths that move us forward in every journey, those breaths that move us across oceans of every kind, away from those we love, to adventures, to our destinies.

My grandfather sailed across the ocean, sailed away from all that was familiar to him from forever, sailed into dreams and hopes of a new world.

He was a stone mason and America needed to be built, so work was easy to find. He was very frugal with his money. He'd sleep under bridges to save on rent. He sacrificed his own comfort day after day, month after month, he vigilantly saved his money and finally sent it to Michelina so that she and Alberto could join him in America.

Michelina was delighted to receive money from Vincenzo. But she, like Vincenzo, certainly wasn't foolish with her money, so of course she didn't buy tickets for passage to America as Vincenzo wanted, she bought more land in Italy instead! She bought more land so that when her son, Alberto, grew up, he would have lots and lots of beautiful land in Italy, where he belonged.

Vincenzo was infuriated when he learned that Michelina had defied him. When he learned she would not join him in America he saved his money with a vengeance and sailed right back across the ocean to Italy to confront her. He was incensed that she could be so stubborn. She was incensed that he could be so stupid. They fought. They made up. They had another baby. For twenty years he went back and forth across the ocean like a migrating bird, hoping to convince Michelina to come to America with him. Each time that he sent money, she bought more land in Italy. Each time back and forth, back and forth.

Each time they would fight. Each time they would make up. Each time they would have another child.

River cloth, sheepskin, sheepskin, sheepskin, bed sheet, scarf . . .

But Vincenzo was a clever man. He would bring trunks full of souvenirs to entice Michelina and his children. He would bring pencils, movie star photos, pictures of Enrico Caruso the famous Opera singer from nearby Naples who sang in America; and Vincenzo brought lots of beautiful scarves, silk scarves, and he would say, "In America, all the women wear beautiful clothes, silks scarves alive with colours, all their clothes alive with colour." He enticed his wife, Michelina, in her white blouse and dark skirt, wrapping a silk scarf around her neck and flattering her till she blushed at his murmurings about how beautiful she looked. His daughters, too, he adorned like angels in rosy, gold-trimmed silken scarves. Come to America, he'd whisper softly, where there is beauty unimaginable, riches for everyone. Shops full of beautiful dresses already made, milk and eggs delivered right to your door. Life is good in America.

Finally, after twenty years, after many trunk-loads of silks and beautiful things from America, the children, now teenagers, wanted to go with their father. Michelina couldn't believe her ears. Alberto, now nearly twenty and ready to be married, wanted to go with his father to America. All her children wanted to go, to leave Italy. To leave the sheep, the hillsides, the olive trees, to leave the house generations of their family had lived in, the house they were each born in, the house Michelina herself had been born in. And so the choice came to Michelina, stay in Italy with her land and her life, or go to America with her children.

And so, they went. A scarf on the clothesline to mark their departure.

River cloth, sheepskin, sheepskin, sheepskin, bed sheet, scarf, Aunt Josie's dress . . .

Everything was different in America. Everything changed. This dress belonged to my Aunt Josie. Her real name was Gisella, but it was changed by the immigration authorities to Josephine — just as my mother, Maria, became Mary, and Angelina became Angie. Aunt Josie was proud of her new name, and her new dress. Look at it, it has wooden buttons, it has a lace collar, it has colour. There's a flower pattern right in the material. What beauty! How different from the plain country clothes of Italy! My mother had new dresses, too. And my Aunt Angie. They didn't have to wear the clothes they had worn in Italy anymore. They didn't have to spin the wool fibers into thread. They bought dresses ready-made, in shops full of beautiful things, exactly as my grandfather had promised.

River cloth, sheepskin, sheepskin, sheepskin, bed sheet, scarf, Aunt Josie's dress, apron . . .

My mother and her sisters all fell in love, they all had homes, they all had families. My Aunt Josie married my Uncle Nick because they worked in the same dressmaking factory together and rode the subway together every day. They couldn't spend that much time together without people talking about them, so they had to get engaged and married. Josie was the eldest sister, so she got married first, then my mother, then Angie. Josie married Nick the tailor and lived upstairs from Angie, who married Nick the carpenter. My mother married my father, Dominick, a businessman. We lived above our store.

The three sisters lived a couple of blocks from each other, and were always getting together to perm each others' hair, to cook, to have coffee, to have supper on Sunday afternoons.

River cloth, sheepskin, sheepskin, sheepskin, bedsheet, scarf, Aunt Josie's dress, apron, slips, bras, girdle . . .

There were lots of girls in our family: my mother and her sisters, then my mother had four girls of her own, my Aunt Angie had another two, and my grandmother lived with us, as well. There were lots of hand washables, lots of feminine underwear to hang out on the line. We'd walk around in our slips, we'd admire each other's panties. And there were bras, lots of bras, because there were so many breasts.

All the kids in our family were breast fed, not privately in a quiet room, but surrounded by a cooing, admiring audience of all the women in the family. A breast-feeding mother was as sacred as a shrine to the Madonna in Church, we kneeled, we worshipped, we lifted our hearts to Heaven. We absolutely loved proud, delicious, luxurious, breasts. We even went bra shopping together. My mother and her sisters, and all of us girls, would be in the dressing room at the lingerie department together, squeezed in tight, while the grown-ups tried on bras and offered opinions and suggestions. My mother liked the ¾ length style bras and she had lots of them. I think she had more bras than Imelda Marcos had shoes.

I assumed all girls were like this, so in love with their underwear, but then I realized that for my family, this fascination was something very special. In Italy, my mother and her sisters hadn't worn bras. The beautiful bras they loved to shop for were magical wonders of the New World, wonders which transformed them, transformed every woman. Bras were the latest in breast technology. These lovely undergarments were as technically magical to my mother and her sisters as computers are to us today.

The girdles, too. All the women in my family were very sensual, and I remember the pleasure they took in sculpting their bodies, never apologetic, never ashamed, always delighted with the lushness of their womanliness, as if they were Michelangelo working with the choicest marble.

River cloth, sheepskin, sheepskin, sheepskin, bed sheet, scarf, Aunt Josie's dress, apron, slips, bras, girdle, silk blouse, white gloves . . .

My sisters and I grew from girlhood to womanhood. We progressed through clothing that grew more and more beautiful. My mother and her sisters, and all of us girls, everyone had beautiful clothes. My grandfather had been right, there were fine clothes for his daughters in America, silk blouses, lace. Beautiful clothes. Scarves even more beautiful than the ones he had brought them so many years ago were ours in abundance. My mother and her sisters became real ladies, respected in our community, and their father was proud of them. No one ever thought even once to ask them if they were daughters of the man whose family lived in a cave. They were respectable. Respected. His daughters, respected.

River cloth, sheepskin, sheepskin, sheepskin, bed sheet, scarf, Aunt Josie's dress, apron, slips, bras, girdle, silk blouse, white gloves, tablecloth . . .

No clothesline from my family would be without a tablecloth, because we were always having company. Come over, they'd say, come over for breakfast after Mass, come over for supper, come over to watch Ed Sullivan. We were always together. We were family. And we had lots and lots of company at our houses, always lots of good food. We couldn't have a gathering without having food. If anyone dropped by, whether invited or unexpected, no matter how difficult it was to feed them, my mother would always say, "I have to give them something." So, time for a lunch break in this story. Let's go to the fridge or the cupboard, take out a little something to enjoy.

But first let's take a moment, please, if you don't mind. Before every meal at home we'd say Grace. We were always eating, but we were always praying, too. So I wrote a prayer for this occasion, just something simple. It's a prayer to Saint Christopher, the Patron Saint of Immigrants.

Saint Christopher, Patron Saint of the Traveller, as a child you played by the river where women washed the family clothes and hung them to dry over bushes. Your mother was there, beating the clothes against the rocks to make them clean, talking to the other mothers about life and death and God and laundry.

Whenever another child needed to cross the river, you carried them because you were a large boy, strong and tall, with a happy heart. You were the ferry man through your youth, all the rest of your life as well. All the women washing laundry agreed it was your calling to help people in their journeys.

So centuries later, when my grandfather boasted of his plan to cross the ocean, even though he could not swim, even though his mind, which had only known the cave of his home, the olives and sheep on sleepy hillsides, could not imagine anything so vast as an ocean much less the crossing of it, you lifted him up and carried him onto the ship, a ship as big as Naples, so he could make his dream of the future come true.

The Atlantic Ocean blessed you with its salted Holy Water. The ship's sails, as white as the veils of girls on the day of their First Communion, sails as white as if beaten against the river rocks by the village women, those sails billowed with the strong wind of many ancient journeys.

Saint Christopher, you carried my grandfather with his heart full of fear and desire; and later you carried my grandmother; and all my aunts and uncles, one by one; my mother, her sheep on the shore calling farewell. Did you know the shores of Italy would never see us again?

Saint Christopher, help of travellers, pray for us.

Saint Christopher, patron saint of immigrants, pray for us.

Saint Christopher, help of the restless heart, hear our prayer.

Now, a little something to eat. *Mangia!* we say in Italian, *Eat!*

At home, there was always a table set with platters of food. Invitations went out so readily for people to come eat with us, meals for any reason at all. Come on over and have coffee, have some pasta, have some soup. Come on over. Come on over. Lots of tablecloths on the clothesline. Have some cheese. Have an olive. More salami?

River cloth, sheepskin, sheepskin, sheepskin, bed sheet, scarf, Aunt Josie's dress, apron, slips, bras, girdle, silk blouse, white gloves, tablecloth, curtain . . .

I remember my grandmother, Michelina, my mother's mother, because she lived with us. She'd sit on the living room couch in the afternoon, gazing out the window, dreaming and sighing. After twenty years of watching her husband go back and forth across the ocean, after twenty years of watching him leave her once again alone in Italy with the children, she had finally followed him to America, giving up all she had, her home, everything. She and the children followed Vincenzo to America in 1929, yes, 1929, the year of the stock market crash. The family struggled in America during the depression, each one working in factories, or as maids, wherever, scraping to get by, only to have Vincenzo die an early death, leaving the family stranded and unable to return to Italy where Michelina's land would have easily taken good care of them all. If Vincenzo weren't already dead, Michelina would have killed him for doing such a thing to her.

I didn't know any of this for decades. What I remember of my grandmother was that she sat on the couch with me in the afternoon sunlight, looking out the window, dreaming of Italy, dreaming of him. She spent a lot of time with me when I was very young. She would speak to me in Italian, which I didn't think I understood, but I realize now that what she was telling me was that there are things about life which go beyond words, which go beyond language, which require understanding.

I would lay my head in her lap and she would sing me a lullaby so I could fall asleep.

Palumello — Butterfly

Semper Vole — Always flying

Cope bracha de nino mio — now on my baby's arm

A ciell'achendere — Up into the sky

Quandi mauro — when I die

Palumma mia, palumma mia — my butterfly, my butterfly

Achende con te — I'll fly with you.

My grandmother died when I was thirteen. But I felt her with me long afterwards. As I grew up and became a woman, married and became a wife and a mother, I felt her presence always. And as the struggles of my life grew, I began to learn about her life, Michelina's life, not just my grandmother's life, but Michelina's life as a woman, as a parent, as a wife whose husband was always leaving. A proud woman embarrassed because the people in the village thought she was crazy to have married a poor man, a man who left her over and over again, a man she loved. And why did he leave, for another woman? When he left, would he return? Michelina couldn't know. Each crossing of the ocean took Vincenzo an entire month. Birds could fly it faster. What was his life like in America? Anything could happen when he wasn't with her at home in Italy.

Michelina's life, my grandmother's story, grew in importance to me as my life unfolded. The comfort she had given in her simple lullaby for me proved an unending source of strength in difficult times. As my understanding of life grew, so did my appreciation and understanding of her. Over time, I realized that if anyone ever needed a lullaby, it was my grandmother. So I wrote one for her, and from time to time, I sing it for her, and I think, wherever she is, whatever ocean she's crossed, she hears it.

River cloth, sheepskin, sheepskin, sheepskin, bed sheet, scarf, Aunt Josie's dress, apron, slips, bras, girdle, silk blouse, white gloves, tablecloth, curtain, hankies . . .

I had two grandmothers, both of them sad.

My father's mother, Antonetta, crocheted and embroidered all the edges on dozens of hankies. She made a lot of them because she cried a lot. She had fallen in love with a man in Italy whose name was Caruso, and he and his brothers had come to America to make their fortunes. Later, when he sent for her, she came from Italy to marry him. But, before they were wed, he was murdered, stabbed to death. Heart-broken, she didn't know what to do. To return to Italy would mean shame. So she did what was the custom of the time, she married her lover's brother, my grandfather, Pasquale. Unfortunately, they hated each other. After their three sons were grown, Antonetta and Pasquale Caruso separated, an unthinkable thing to do as Catholics of their time.

So Grandma Caruso crocheted and embroidered these hankies, dozens of them, maybe hundreds of them, because she was always crying, she was always sad. We'd go visit her, and she'd cook pasta for us. She didn't speak English, only Italian, so she'd never talk, but as we were leaving she'd say her one English phrase, *so long*, and talk and talk and talk in Italian, to me especially, because I was so short, I think, talk to me in Italian, wanting, I think, not to impart facts, but rather, begging for understanding about the sadness she felt in missing Italy, the sadness she felt about her life.

River cloth, sheepskin, sheepskin, sheepskin, bed sheet, scarf, Aunt Josie's dress, apron, slips, bras, girdle, silk blouse, white gloves, tablecloth, curtain, hankies, baby quilt . . .

Time went on. The grandchildren grew, and sometimes made the grandparents smile. As I said, I was thirteen when my grandmother Michelina died; all of us grandchildren were young when the old ones passed away. All of them died within days of each other. It was like the parish ran a bus tour to Heaven, and they had all bought tickets to travel together. While our grandparents were alive, I don't think any of us really knew their stories or had a sense of our own family history, and even today, most of us have never even been to Italy, to the place our grandparents and parents called home all their lives, even long after they had left.

But this much I know: no one ever intended to make anyone unhappy. No one intended to hurt anyone — ever. They were following their dreams, my grandfathers; Vincenzo wanted to be worthy of Michelina. Pasquale wanted to honour his brother.

My grandmothers, they were following their men. They were dreaming of a life, a good life, together. Michelina always felt that someday Vincenzo would stay home with her where he belonged, and when he didn't, she left everything to be with him. Antonetta sailed alone across an ocean for the man she loved.

They were all sailing on ships and dreaming of a better life. Not once did they dream of causing pain. They didn't envision sighs and tears and loneliness and longing. They had no idea what price would be paid, or what rewards there would be. Who knew what fortunes awaited them?

In the New World, my grandfather, Vincenzo, loved to linger in the alleyway by the opera house to listen at the stage door. To hear Enrico Caruso sing transported him as close to Heaven as he thought possible on this Earth. But for all the dreams Vincenzo ever dreamed, had he ever dared to dream that one of his own daughters would marry into the family of the Great Caruso? That, exactly that, is what came about, Vincenzo dreamed, Vincenzo journeyed, and Dominick Caruso, my father, met and married Maria, my mother, Vincenzo's daughter, who crossed the ocean with Vincenzo on his ship of dreams. Destinies were unfolding: the destinies of dreamers.

As I walk back and forth behind this clothesline, I watch the breeze lift the clothes up into the sunshine like a sacred offering. All my life, I've walked beside this clothesline, lain under it, listened to familiar voices tell this story. These stories of dreams and trust and journeys, these stories of old customs in new lands, these stories of mismatched matches, of life companions who are never there — this is what I know, this is what I write about; these people who speak a foreign language are the ones I understand. They who dreamed of happiness, yet made the people they loved unhappy, it's their story I tell.

The river near Conca a la Compagna still flows. The village women still wash their clothes in it, pounding sheets and shirts against the rocks until they are clean again. The river water remembers its own forever and seeks to sanctify. It evaporates up into the sky above Conca, and forms clouds. The clouds, blown by the wind, by the breath of dreams, sail across the vastness of the ocean, across mountains, across valleys, across continents, finding us wherever we are. Those clouds rain down the waters from the river at Conca and bless each one of us, baptizing us with the Holy Water, washing us clean, baptizing us as family, no matter where on this earth we are.

I know this because I see it written in my flesh. See this line in my palm, this lifeline? It is this clothesline, my bloodline, the clothesline of my lineage. There in my flesh, in my DNA, in the very palm I extend in greeting, in the very hand with which I write these stories, engraved there forever, forever and ever.

This story, my story.

All I ask is this: when I die, add me to this clothesline story. Add my sighs and hopes and dreams to the stories of my lineage. Make this laundry story which has been my life, become my final resting place. Make this clothesline my shroud.

PALUMELLO

ON HER DRESSER, THE VIGIL LIGHT FLICKERED in front of the picture of Mother Cabrini. I stood on tip toe and inhaled the holy scent of the beeswax candle carefully, so as not to disturb the flame with my breath. I dipped my finger into the warm, melted wax and lifted it up into the cool air to watch it cloud over and harden into a perfect veil — not unlike the one Mother Cabrini wore in her picture, not unlike what women wore in church.

It was long ago, when I was only a girl, and my grandmother, Michelina, was living in my parents' house. I heard her call:

Dona Maria, veni ca.

Donna Marie, come here.

Va dormi, va dormi, Dona Maria!

Go to sleep, go to sleep.

My grandmother would sit on the couch in the afternoon, and I would lie next to her with my head in her lap. I was three. I spoke no Italian, her only tongue; but somehow I could understand her every word. She told me of Mother Cabrini's miracles, ones she had witnessed herself.

Like the time an overpowering smell of roses filled the house all day long, when there was in fact only one rose in the house. A blood red one, in front of Mother Cabrini's picture. It was the middle of winter. The same day the letter from Italy came telling my grandma of her mother's death. She knew from the smell of the roses that her mother was with Mother Cabrini in Heaven. It was a sign. It kept her heart from breaking.

Nona nona, she sang, *filia mia va dormi.*

Her lullaby for me. She would ever so gently rock her legs back and forth, singing and singing, until the world fell away and I was sound asleep.

Outdoors in summer, she would sit in the sunshine, in her hand a glass sugar jar, an inch of sugar in the bottom. I would be over on the grass watching the bees dancing on the flower tops.

Dona Maria, veni ca.

A butterfly would light on the sugar, and she would slip the lid onto the jar, then hold it in the sunlight for me to see. We would look at the creature in awe. See it shimmering and happy, then free again, fluttering off, like a house guest after Sunday dinner warm with love and food.

Palumello . . .

Butterfly, she would sing . . .

Semper vole . . .

Always flying . . .

Gope bracha de nina mia . . .

Now on the arms of my baby . . .

A ciell' achendere . . .

Up into the sky . . .

Quandi mauro . . .

When I die . . .

Paluma mia, paluma mia, Io 'scende con te.

My butterfly, my butterfly, I'll fly with you.

There was an old photograph she had, formal and posed. In it, she stood next to a small man. She was straighter than he; taller. They looked ahead, separate, unsmiling. It was taken on their wedding anniversary.

She held the photograph for me to see as we sat on the couch, the streams of afternoon sunlight making my eyelids heavy with sleep. Again and again she would look from the photo off into space, to the world of her memories, then back again. The story was there in the photo, and there in her sighs. It was a private story, full of love and hope, of disappointment and pain. Full of too many things for a little girl to understand.

Back in my actual time with her, when she gently stroked my hair and coaxed me to sleep, all I understood was, "This was your grandpa. He died before you were born." But later, many years later, after she, too, was gone, I was haunted by her story, silent yet indelible, written on the walls of my memory.

In the evening every Friday, she watched the fights on TV as religiously as she tended the vigil light before Mother Cabrini's picture in her room. I sat beside her on the couch. The TV picture was black and white in those days, the men black and white as well. Such fascinating men, in their fancy underwear, hitting each other week after week. Spitting in their corners, sweating, bleeding — their large feet danced as they circled each other, then charged. Fists connected so squarely, I could feel the pain myself.

As we sat together quietly on the couch, never cheering lest we disturb someone, we spent the hour wide-eyed, captivated by the shirtless men in the box. She may have spoken no English, but she understood the language of the fights, as did I. Grandma and I spoke fluent "Friday Night Fights".

Saturday afternoon there was wrestling. Grandma and I watched that, too. But it was my nap time, so I drifted off to sleep as Wild Man was about to pounce on Red Devil, the midget tag team about to attack the Giant.

I would eventually go to school, the Catholic school, run by nuns who obviously were as enamored of the Friday Night Fights and wrestling as my grandmother and I. Anything but shirtless and sweaty, they nonetheless knew the power of a quick right to the jaw and the righteousness of a solid headlock.

My grandmother carried her rosary with her always, just as the nuns did. She would sit for hours fingering the beads, petitioning Heaven . . .

Baggi la groce.

Kiss the cross, she would entreat me in Italian. *Kiss the cross.* I would kiss the metal crucifix, warm with the heat of my grandmother's hands. It was Jesus, the Son of God, she said. I remember wondering if Jesus, Son of God, was ever on the Friday Night Fights.

In the other old photograph she had, she sat with her four living children, unbelievably young, standing around her. My mother barely two. It was taken long ago in the days before candid photography, back when every photo was serious and painfully posed, with the children in unfamiliar and stiff clothing and shoes that pinched. No wonder everyone was unsmiling.

There was no man in the picture. The photograph would have been taken in Italy to be sent to Grandpa across the ocean. He had left his wife and babies in Italy while he worked in the new world, where he felt there was opportunity unlike any other. For twenty years he went back and forth and back and forth across the ocean like a migrating bird, while she was free to raise her children alone. But she was never angry, not when I knew her.

Each morning she would braid up her waist-length hair into a bun and fasten it with long, dark pins. I would stand by her side as, unhurried, she brushed, then braided. The vigil light before Mother Cabrini's picture felt warm on my face as I watched the ritual. The aroma of my grandma's hair cream, mixed with the smell of the bees wax candle created a sense of holiness, the special shrine of my grandmother.

She rarely spoke, so each word seemed as sacred as a blessing.

Io te ho cucinato un po di pastina. Mange! Mange!

I made you some pastina she would say as she put the bowl, filled with pasta stars and laced with olive oil, before me. My mother fed me Cheerios. Grandma fed me stars. Surely the woman came from Heaven if this is what she fed small children for breakfast.

She herself never ate, except for the occasional lamb chop or bowl of homemade soup or piece of fresh fruit. While I ate my pastina, she would stand looking out the window. We were on the second floor, over my parents' store. The kitchen faced the backyard, where there were large fruit trees and rows of my father's lush rosebushes. Birds rested on the telephone wires and paused in their flight across the huge, blue sky. Bees danced on the yellow heads of the dandelions.

We would go out onto the small, second-storey back porch to hang out the wash after breakfast, and I would smell the clean white sheets as she hung them on the line in the breeze. They would billow, once released, like a ship's sail on the ocean. She had crossed an ocean as blue and as vast as the sky to live here with that small dark man in the photograph. The journey had taken nine long days. She must have wondered if the sails that brought her here would ever take her home.

My grandmother and I would sit together on that small back porch enjoying the morning sunshine, high above the yard, and look out over the neighbourhood. Our laundry sailed above that of the neighbours and made us feel like the front runners in an important regatta. Ours was the highest clothesline, the longest clothesline, and easily the most spirited. Where we were headed was less important than that we were sailing.

In reality, we were the least likely of sailors. She had had too much of the ocean already in coming over from Italy, and I was hardly buoyant, even though I was a toddler. I wore a heavy plaster cast which covered me completely from my waist to my ankles. It had the colour of the white sheets on the line, but nothing of the spirit. My shell for a full year, it was the reason my grandmother spent so much time with me. Unlike the others, who were free to go when they liked, I stayed with her, and she stayed with me. For years. She was the old and foreign one; I, a crippled toddler. We didn't matter to anyone and nobody listened to us but, for one another, day by day, we made life wonderful and mysterious.

Sometimes, the other family members would bring the wild western culture home with a bang. From our usual station, the couch, she and I would watch whatever we could not or would not take part in.

Mambo lessons come to mind.

The music was as hot as the Latin countries from which it had sprung. My parents, my aunts and uncles, and seemingly all of their friends wanted to learn this and other exuberant dances. The living room, which usually seemed large enough in the quiet afternoons when just my grandmother and I were there, seemed dangerously inadequate to hold all the enthusiastic dancers invading the house every Sunday night with their loud and pulsating music.

Among those sounding the doorbell was the mambo instructor, a man with shiny shoes and slicked back hair. He made the dancers pair off and learn new steps for an hour, then left them to practice on their own. These practices were what really cemented the relationship between my grandmother and me.

Setta ca.

Sit here, she would entreat me as the dancing began. I was only too happy to oblige her by climbing on the couch beside her and snuggling close.

Neither of us could move too quickly; I because of the heavy, unwieldy plaster cast, and she because of the age in her joints. If it became apparent we were no longer safe on the couch — which usually was made clear after someone's circle skirt had spun in our faces, or someone had landed in our laps — then it was no easy task to make it past the dancers. We would tightly hold the other's hand, each of us staggering in our own way, as plodding as the dancers were graceful.

In the safety of my grandma's room, we would lie down on her bed, and watch the flickering of the vigil light. Mother Cabrini's face was always serene no matter what the circumstances. The vigil light a soft, flickering glow contrasting with the fire of music and dance which consumed the living room. Grandma would sing to me:

Palumello . . .

Butterfly . . .

I could hear the mambo music in the parlour . . . .

Semper vole . . .

Always flying . . .

Looking up at her I could see her eyes were sad . . .

Gope bracha de nina mia . . .

Now on the arms of my baby . . .

She covered me with the edge of her blanket and stroked my arm . . .

A ciell' achendere . . .

Up into the sky . . .

Quandi mauro . . .
When I die . . .
My eyes would grow heavy, and I would sleep . . .
Paluma mia, paluma mia, Io 'scende con te . . .
My butterfly, my butterfly, I'll fly with you.

I was thirteen when she died. The day of her burial in late December most bitterly cold. We lined up, dozens of us, her descendants, her family, and one by one we were handed a cool, long-stemmed, blood-red rose to throw into her grave, onto her coffin.

As I approached the open pit — a place too cold for anything but death — and was about to let fall my rose, the smell of roses lifted like a sweet incense through the icy air. A smell of roses so strong, I knew it was a sign, a sign she had joined all the other daughters of roses in Heaven.

Now, as my life unfolds, I find I decipher more of hers. The messages in childhood memories, once cryptic, now shine clear and intelligible. Her language, my own.

Markers Of History

Hansel and Gretel left breadcrumbs. Arthur Murray left dance prints. My mother and her sisters left the red lipstick imprint of kisses to mark the path of their lives. Aunt Angie left them on our cheeks, big, sticky, perfect smooches. Bright red, as vibrant as the smile she smiled at us afterwards as she smeared the kisses with her thumb so that they rosied-up our cheeks like rouge. Aunt Angie's kisses left us looking healthy and happy.

Aunt Josie wasn't much of a kisser, she was a cook. And when her food was good enough to serve to us, she kissed her fingertips and saluted Heaven for blessing her efforts. Heaven stationed a legion of angels around Aunt Josie to bless her and the food that came from her hands, to make her smile sparkle.

My mother's red lips pressed a perfect imprint onto a folded Kleenex which she held delicately as she smiled at her reflection in the mirror. When she kissed our cheeks, the imprint was faint, hardly a stroke needed to erase its whisper of a mark. In photos of her, she smiles warmly, rightly, exactly with the vibration of the red on her lips. Her colour, always, red.

The family photo albums bloom with those red-lipped kisses. Snapshots show us growing up, fed with the kisses Aunt Josie sent to Heaven, rosied by the kisses Aunt Angie rubbed into our cheeks, and matured by the lady-like smiles of our mother.

Some family heritages can be traced through military rankings, or public offices, or Heads of State; some through rice paddies, vineyards, or farmlands. Our map of red kisses dances through time, attentive to every detail, marking the sacred, the celebratory, the departed, as natural as song to the angels.

True Romans In the Family Album

A meditation on a photograph

IN THE PHOTO I DISCOVERED LONG AFTER his parting, my grandfather sat on the trunk of the big old Chrysler with Jimmy, his lifelong friend. Two well seasoned guys, cigar stubs as always in their smiling mouths. They had grown up in Italy together, crossed the ocean together, saw the New World with their young men's eyes, and dreamed together about life in the New World. In fact, their whole lives they had shared their dreams, from the time they were boys till now as old men where they sat, smoking, on the Chrysler.

Italian immigrants in the early 1900s, their youth was spent spinning ocean-sized dreams of fabulous opportunity that would amaze the villagers left behind to tend sheep and olive groves on the Italian hillsides. Their dreams rose like the cigar smoke, floating wreaths of possibility up, up, up like prayers, like kisses from young virgins, full of innocence and hope. These two could not live without dreaming. Their hearts, minds, and souls dreamed grandeur into all things, every day things. And in the New World, there were so many dreams to dream, far more than in Italy, where the ancestors had dreamed all the dreams long ago. The New World was wild with available dreams. They could own houses, and they did, houses with enormous gardens; they could own cars, and they did, with chrome bumpers and white walled tires; and each owned a shop, a shop that bore their own name. There were parades, festivals, and *new* women — not women they had known since birth like the girls in the village back home.

But even if that weren't so, they would have dreamed. It was their way. It was their passion. They dreamed as they breathed, for life itself, to transform life itself.

Just as the Romans of old had envisioned the excellence of something as basic as a road, so too had these Roman descendants inherited the gene for dreaming the grand and glorious version of every ordinary thing, of every moment of ordinary life. It was the legacy of their heritage written on the walls of their hearts.

You could see it, a sparkle crackling like halos about their heads, the dancing of dreams in there, the shimmers of possibility in their eyes. Such alive eyes. The eyes of boys free in summer to roam the countryside of Italy and, later, the oceans of the world. They knew, these two, that whatever else may happen to them in their lives, they had found in each other someone who understood their love of dreaming.

True Romans, proud in their heart of hearts, empire builders no matter whether they made wine, or played cards, or just sat outside and smoked. Their dreaming went on, infusing everything with glory, love, and lusciousness, so disappointment could never for a moment take hold. A thousand things they would do in a day, from pouring a glass of wine to admiring a rose. Always they dreamed the grandest and loveliest into being, dreamed the best of all possible glasses of wine, the most beautiful of all roses. The peppers and tomatoes in their gardens stood in the straightest rows, the homemade vinegar on their salads blended perfectly with the olive oil. Oil like chrism used by the priest, to anoint and to confirm.

See them — smiling, smoking, the ocean in their eyes, the sky there, too. Fig trees and sheep on the hillsides in Italy still smile at the memory of their boyhood. The lives of two relentless dreamers woven through with the prayers of their mothers and the smiles of ancient emperors. In the end, Heaven was glad to have them back, for truly, they never left.

Nick Caruso's Nose

My uncle, Nick Caruso, had a nose as big as the Carlsbad caverns. As a child I was fascinated. As a teenager, I imagined whole civilizations arose, prospered, and vanished within the resonances of Uncle Nick's hallowed nose. My father's older brother, Uncle Nick sat with us around our dining room table, as regal as the Sphinx, the strong, enormous man with the magnificent, exquisite nose.

His thighs were as thick as the cedars of Japanese temple gates, and he was a tall man, taller than all the rest of the family by far, his spine straight as a signal tower, his massive head the beacon seen for leagues across the landscape. Uncle Nick's broad bald head, never covered with much hair even in his youngest days, glistened the way granite glistens, glinting at you secretly in the corner of your eye.

He dressed in black, drove a black Cadillac, and wore a black fedora, the brim pulled forward a bit to accentuate the nose of noses. His prominent and chiseled Roman features surely spoke of a lineage of gladiators, emperors, and sons of gods. Jupiter himself could have claimed him as progeny. As it was, Nick was the eldest son of a shoemaker; the eldest of three sons: Nick, Dominick, and Louie.

During the Second World War, Nick went off prepared to fight in the trenches, but served in the Pacific, stationed on an island where the women walked around bare-breasted. Apparently, no shots were fired anywhere near where Nick was stationed and he came home a happy man. He had carried no rabbit's foot, no four leaf clover. Some people are born under a lucky star, some people take lemons and make lemonade, some, they say, just have a nose for good fortune.

Nick was a surprisingly sweet man. On Mother's Day, he would stand outside his mother's third floor walk-up, knocking, holding a blue hydrangea, calling to her, "Ma, Ma, it's Nick." In her apron, she would open the door, exclaiming welcomes in Italian. An impossibly small woman with sorrowful eyes, she always smiled at her sons, and particularly, she always smiled at Nick. Some say it was because he was her eldest son, her first born. But it was his nose that made her smile, how could it not be?

For though Grandma Caruso lost everything precious to her when she left Italy, as long as she could see that nose of Nick's, she could see Vesuvius, she could see a reminder of the Italian mountaintop where her village stood. In this strange land she'd come to, so different from the home within her heart, reminders of home were rare and most welcome.

And if Grandma Caruso stood on her tall son Nick's broad shoulders, steadying herself by hanging onto that sturdy nose of his, she could see all the way across the ocean past the church steeple in the town square to the pasture where she had grazed her goats, to the hillsides where, as a girl, she had dreamed a life so different than what this one turned out to be.

Nick's nose held the secret hopes of Grandma. No one ever made a crack about it, no derisive jokes, not even a thought to diminish its merit.

Uncle Nick Caruso's nose was a beacon of light pointing towards home, towards the greatness of Roman ancestors, artists, builders, and explorers, the centuries' long lineage of beauty that made us as Italians proud. In the New World, we needed to be reminded of our heritage, especially at those times when things were said against us because we were dark. Southern Italians like my family saw plenty of prejudice. But Uncle Nick's Roman nose went both ways, outward to past glory, and inward to the inherent strength of our line. Our ancestors had built cathedrals, roads, viaducts — Italy is full of their work — stone tunnels and bridges, statues of saints and emperors. Those statues preserved our Romanesque physiques through millennia, including our excellent noses. Uncle Nick's nose was an especially fine specimen. Noses like his are what make us proud no matter what.

The Lions Of Rome

Eyes full of fire, angry jaws wide with roaring, the lions of Rome ate Christians for breakfast, Christians for lunch, Christians for supper. They must have complained about the Coliseum fare. They must have complained about the scrawny, bony, Christian tissue marinated in juices bitter with fear from too long a contemplation of death by lion. Give us gazelles, cried the lions of Rome, plump gazelles grazing on the sweet grass of Africa, gazelles whose graceful leap is a leap of faith. You force these doomed Christians upon us. Who wants this puny prey?

Sometime later, when Popes built palaces neighbouring the Coliseum, palaces buttressed by the bones of those martyred Christians, the Curia commissioned sculptors to carve guardian lions for the Papal gates, civilized lions tamed by the blood of the innocent, jaws silenced, paws extended in friendship.

Today, sons and daughters of Italian immigrants return to Rome as tourists to sip cappuccino in outdoor cafés. The language of their mothers and fathers foreign to them, the food of their ancestors exotic on their tongues, they throw coins into ancient fountains, deeply-rooted wishes in their hearts, wishes arising from the New World graves of their fathers and mothers, wishes as desperate as any prayers from the Coliseum.

Antiquity hangs in the air like clouds on the gentle winds, time folds and fans and folds again. Immigrants of long ago left these shores full of hope, the echoes of their farewells forever on the tide, diffusive in the air. To unknowing offspring they bequeathed their longing to return. Their hopes still rise and fade like the Coliseum's crowds of old. Caesar, Christ, Caligula, the mighty and the mad, having once breathed and bled, breathe and bleed evermore.

The Lions of Rome thunder their agony in their own immigrant roars and rumbling silences, their pleas for the pleasure of gazelles etched eternally on the walls of time and space . . . *how far is Rome from Africa?* Their pleas rise with the prayers and wishes, *How far the plains of home?*

Lingua Familia

My mother stood at the stove, stirring. She glanced at the clock over the sink, waiting for my father to come upstairs for supper. The table was set for seven — my parents and us five kids — forks, knives and spoons set formally, napkins folded under the fork. My sisters and I prepared the space, the delicious smells of dinner making us hungrier as we worked, one getting the silverware, one the plates, one the napkins, another pulling the table out from the wall and clearing it off. *Life* magazine was moved aside, the table wiped clean, the glasses set for red wine. Chianti in a straw-bottomed bottle emerged cool from the pantry. The gallon-size wine bottle, corked after each meal, generally lasted a week or more. Everyone drank wine. A glass even for the youngest. Just a little, in ginger ale sometimes, especially when it was hot in summer.

With a long-handled spoon, my mother gently lifted the macaroni to keep it from sticking to the bowl, a yellow pottery bowl with floral trim, the bowl warm in the oven, warm with the memories of decades of ziti and marinara sauce. Meatballs and sausage ladled along one side like a mountain range ready for Hannibal. Everything waited until my father climbed the stairs from our store where he worked from nine in the morning until ten at night, six days a week.

He came upstairs for all his meals. When he was delayed, like tonight, supper waited. My mother waited, we all waited, the aromas of my mother's delicious Italian meals drifted in a slow dance through the house, enticing us, making our stomachs ache with longing.

My father's footfalls on the stairs were a dinner bell which signaled our migration to the kitchen. My mother stood at the table and spooned portions onto our plates as we took our places, my father at the head, my brother opposite him, we girls and my mother along the sides. Glasses were passed for the wine, and, settling down with food and drink before us, we all said Grace.

Every meal was blessed. The words rose as the steam rose from our supper, our ziti incense, headed up to Heaven where God no doubt heard our prayer, smelled our food, and seeing we were good and grateful, sat at my father's right hand as if he belonged in our family, as if he, too, were grateful for a good supper.

The Human Genome Project: Lineages

Our roots follow those of the olive trees, deep into dark Vesuvian soil. Our ancestors reclined, hidden by olive-scented branches to kiss to couple to become who we are, a people whose fire pits and graves lay side by side, whose peaceful sheep huddle close by without worry, knowing each day the hillsides and green grass will abound with love and humming in the sunlight.

Dark eyes and hair from this rich earth rise again and again in each generation, olives in the skin tone, oil on the lips to kiss to taste to call by name, familial language song of songs where ancient and eternal life is written on the intestinal wall.

A fingerprint of volcanic soil on the forehead marks the people of this land. Tomatoes grown from seeds licked by the lions of Rome cook as ever over the fire. Draw water from the river and pour it into jugs, fill the glasses first with water then with wine, to drink, to nourish the blood.

Rocks jiggle up from the earth's core steaming, ready for the journey to sand, to beach, to pearl. Accordion chord progressions and harmonic blends pitch and roll, confident sheep sing like Caruso and the countryside chorus unfolds endlessly with voices in ancient harmony.

The sea below this landscape slips against the shore like a lover in the night, wanting to spirit away the people in dream-ships to distant shores for more dreamings in other tongues for more exotic couplings.

The sea wants always to bring us elsewhere, beats against us like a persistent child saying let's go now let's go now, and waves of us — waves of us — left the sheep on the hillside, left the olives in the groves, and sailed away from our bread crumb trail, sailed away on dreams, sailed away on seawater, away from the blood of our ancestors, from the land that fed us, the land we called home, unaware that the salty sea of blood in our veins would call to us forever as well, to return, always to return, and we would never leave off hearing that call even though we would never be able to answer it.

The ocean's salt air enters our lungs and salts us all against our will, salt water vapour mixing with our blood so that even our hidden places taste of the sea now. How different our breasts must taste to our children born here in the land of foreigners, how different our breasts from our mothers and grandmothers, how salty the milk suckling our sons and daughters. *This is my Body* . . . To taste us would even our own grandmothers know us as family?

There are no olives here, no sheep, no hillsides. To build our future we have only memories and dreams. The sea is one-way and brings us only and evermore here, to clanging cities devoid of singing sheep. Here we have house cats, and Pekinese dogs unable to smile. Here we have Cheezies. The hillsides are jammed with traffic and even the Lamb of God would give up hope here.

We have released our children onto ice floes, who knows where they will wind up, or whether winter will ever end. They had friends in the old country, friends for life, birth till death. The memory of friendship is all they have here. Who has the time to explain to anyone who we are or what we have lived?

These are nice people, yes, but not of our bones. The people of our bones stayed on the shore.

My grandmother wept every day. Praying to Saint Anthony, the patron saint of lost articles, she prayed for her lost home. And even though Saint Anthony found everything else, like keys and gloves and wallets and rosaries, even he could not find her home again.

OLIVES ET AL CHEEZIES TO GO

MY MOTHER TENDED SHEEP ON THE HILLSIDES of Southern Italy where the olive groves still grow. Each fall, the tiny olive trees shed their leaves, and those leaves enriched the soil for the next generation of olives. Generations of my family and generations of olive trees, olives beautiful and bountiful in their sustenance. It was our way, the pattern of trees on the hillside, the branches of olives, the leaves falling to earth and rising again in the next olives, food for generations of our family.

When my mother's family kissed the sheep goodbye and set out for the New World, the hillsides of olive trees remained in Italy, their roots too deep, too embedded in the soil which held all record of time and history and life and which fed the future.

Today, I live in the New World, rootless, transplanted far from the life my ancestors knew, far from the land which fed them for generations. I rake my New World leaves around this house on New World soil and in the leaf pile I find litter — this time it's an empty Cheezies bag. When my family came here long ago from Italy, it was BC, Before Cheezies, as it were. The aunts, the uncles, the grandmothers and grandfathers, the cousins, all came. Every one in turn stepped off the soil where the olives grew and onto the boat bound for foreign shores. I wonder if I will ever know what dream lay in their hearts. I wonder if they had any idea that they were trading olives for Cheezies.

This Cheezies bag is cellophane, the Cheezies may be, too. The olives bear more resemblance to my mother than they do to these Cheezies, the olives grown in soil distilled from the bones of my ancestors, from their dreams and their stories, from their legacies, from their feasts and their sorrows. I have to ask the ones who immigrated, what else did you trade without knowing?

I long for the comfort of my family's sheep. I long for the soil that held the bones of my people to antiquity, and the manna of olives they fed me. These Cheezies come from nobody's people. To eat what grows from the earth, from soil familiar to the body and blood of our kin is a holy thing. To eat Cheezies, to eat what has no relevance to our earthly flesh, brings madness.

But this need to migrate is a hunger from the very core of Mother Earth, from the white hot boiling in her lava centre that is her howling blood. Hear her in the call of the snow geese in spring and fall. Feel her in the stampedes of the herds over the plains. Her song, written in the thump of our restless hearts, calls us ever forward, like a vow, in sickness and in health, till death do us part. The rhythm of our bloodstream her imprint, her desire to escape, stamped into our every fibre, her molten mother's milk fed to our every cell. We feel it in the seductive brightness of the surface, the allure of the horizon, the madness of hopes and dreams — all visions of the gods that were the core of the life force at the beginning.

My grandfather got on a boat for an inexplicable journey away from the figs and the olives and the sheep, the village women left behind to weep in the churchyard, the desolate mourning of his parents rising from their graves. No doubt my grandfather's heart beat hard with excitement, no doubt his eyes shown bright with delight and desire, no doubt the thrill of the boat ride and the flow of his journey carried me along with him, at least thus far, abruptly to end when this bag of Cheezies emerged from the fall leaves, a message in a bottle asking if I'd noticed the price of land in the New World and if I'd seen the faces of my relatives on the rows and rows of headstones at the graveyard.

Ellis Island lists the roll call, ships' rosters, immigration records, land titles offices, town hall files. The tears of first and second generation fall, their keening fills the night sky. Where will you be tomorrow my little ones who were raised on Cheezies? Will the olives grow there? Will the olives grow there? Will the olives grow there?

Our Father

The House On Main Street

Traffic slowed to watch the salvage operation of the hundred year old house. The insides were being deconstructed piece by piece, planks laid bare, timbers taken away to the truck out front, studs revealed, private areas opened to public view. I slowed, too, searching the work site — the "For Sale" sign marked "Sold"; the side door, the kitchen door, the front door, all doors wide open; ladders and men inside and out, strong old timbers in sunlight for the first time in over one hundred years. The caragana hedge once wonderfully tall in front of the house, now shorn right down for the wreckers' easy access to the street. My boys and I had lived there at 302 Main Street after the divorce. Cleaned it, fixed it up, and bought a happy young dog at the flea market to move in with us.

We had watched parades from the upstairs window, a window which looked out onto Main Street like the crow's nest of a sailing ship. It seemed we were always looking out from that comforting old house, to an endlessly inviting and pleasant world. I looked to our old home as I often had, a touchstone, a gateway to memories I loved. Then a shock as startling as a magician's trick, as awful as a suddenly missing wedding ring — I noticed the old beauties, the stained glass windows, were gone.

The sunlight through the coloured glass had fallen on my young sons' cheeks each time that they had climbed those stairs. I could see the roses and creams of the glass-filtered sun on their faces, even with my boys gone, and the windows gone as well. Once, in July, the temperature was so hot our candles on the sill of the big stained glass window in the living room melted from the heat, melted without being lit. Bent right over with the heat, as if *Swan Lake* were playing and they bowed in the finale of the corps de ballet.

The road was crunchy with debris from the house, dismantling being as careless and messy a job as homemaking is careful and tidying. A one-ton truck, an old one, with a red wooden box and blue cab, stood guard in front of the house. A man stood beside it looking at 302 Main Street, his face deeply creased and tanned, his cap held tight in thick fingers. The house seemed to look back with empty eyes. The traffic resumed normal speed.

I thought of my father, Dominick, two thousand miles away, who in the evenings, studied the map and wondered why I had moved to a different country, away from the home of my childhood. He was sick at that time with cancer. Not a raging, galloping cancer. Just a small, meandering cancer, which annoyed him, and made him so uncharacteristically tired; gave him more of an inclination to sit in his big old green chair in the living room, to look at maps, gaze out the window, and wonder about why I was so far away.

When I was small, the windows in my father's home looked out from the second storey over his grocery store where he worked every day but Sunday. My bedroom overlooked a yard where an enormous, lone cherry tree stood in the lush green of the neighbour's expansive lawn. A gentle giant, it flowered in spring with the delicacy of its kind, but because of its huge size it seemed surreal, its pink petals falling in spring like the softest sweetest rain on earth, a young girl's rain; and I felt kissed by angels whenever I saw it.

Downstairs in the store, my father would work long days, smiling broadly, greeting his customers like old friends, stocking his shelves, and directing his loyal workers. It was an era when pride, not greed, was paramount; and for my father, an immigrant from Italy, a time of tremendous gratitude for his good fortune. I felt safe there in his house. The whole world looked safe when I looked out his windows.

Trees guarded my father's house, in the same way stone lions had guarded his father's. The cherry tree next door, the mulberry in our yard. Sweet fruit trees, but higher than a house, even higher than a tall house like ours with a store below it. Amazing trees, seemingly ancient giants, wondrous and protective.

We would climb the mulberry tree in the backyard, three or four of us at a time, a large, generous tree, a tree like a big happy woman with a large lap, holding us children securely as we twisted and sat. We would call to people below us, hidden in the tree's abundant foliage, and watch them look around and finally up to us, smiling when they saw us. "Come up!" we'd say, "Come on up and join us!" The adults never would, though we could tell they'd like to; but kids did, and we'd crowd together in the arms of our tree.

My two boys and all the neighbourhood kids had played in the spacious back yard of the house on Main Street, a treeless backyard in a Saskatchewan prairie town. They'd gather for soccer, the goals being the rabbit cage at one end and the old canoe at the other. The rabbits would watch, terrified, hiding in the enclosed part each time the boys would scramble near them; hopping out, curious, when the ball was booted around at the other end of the yard. When the boys stopped to catch their breath, they'd feed the rabbits long green grass, stooping down, speaking to them softly, reassuring them that they were not in danger.

The gulls would come on Sunday mornings, early, before anyone had ventured out to church. They'd land, then walk purposefully, in the middle of the road, as if reclaiming it as theirs and reminding us this land was for use only by leave of their graciousness. They would always choose the centre of the road, not the sidewalks or the parking lots. Strutting slowly, proudly, as silent as if they were in church, the gull parade was like the other parades we watched from that house, but more dignified, with greater purpose and far more decorum. Where the gulls went after Sunday morning no one knew; we never saw them otherwise. They must have been somewhere, watching, waiting, like the rabbits, waiting for the hubbub to die down so they could venture out.

When I lived at my father's house over the store, we would drive on Sunday afternoons in summer to see the gulls flying over the ocean, screaming as they swooped to catch fish. We would drive, five children and my parents, to the bay by the ocean, the salty air cleansing, clearing our lungs and reddening our cheeks. The gulls would cry out, noisy as car horns in traffic jams, displeased about something — not enough blue in the sky, too much salt in the air — they cried and screeched unceasingly as my father rented a row boat for the day.

We would carefully climb on board the rented boat, my mother ordering us to sit still, terrified as she was of the water ever since her long ocean voyage from Italy in her youth. My father would row out past the gulls to where the crab beds lay, bushel baskets lined with seaweed on the floor of the boat before him.

"This is far enough", my mother would implore, but he would row on, enjoying the pull of the oars across the water. If we never stopped he would be delighted just to row, his strong arms happiest at work; like Noah with his family in the ark, saving us, bringing us to a place that God had whispered in his ear. Out beyond where the gulls screamed, where it was quiet, and solitary, he would stop, resting the dripping oars beside us in the boat. And we would cast in our lines, baited with chunks of fish to entice the crabs, silent so as not to scare them away. The water would lap at the side of the boat as we waited, so excited in our silent vigil.

The crabs we caught would come up hissing, snapping their claws, swinging wildly from the end of our lines, wonderfully terrifying. We would scream and try to get away, the boat shaking, my mother calling out in panic, afraid we would tip, afraid she and her five fearful children would wind up in the deep, briny home of the crabs. But my father would swoop his long strong arm up behind each fighting new-caught crab, amazing us as he grabbed it where the pincers couldn't reach. He'd clutch the smooth shell firmly, an act of bravery astounding to us each time, and drop the crabs one by one into the bushel baskets, where, with the arrival of every newcomer, all the other crabs would skitter and snap, afraid of my father all over again.

Even at eighty, my father could still have rowed a boatful of us, his arms, his heart, far stronger than many men a third his age. He would have been happy to row his family out to the crab beds, to save us again from the snapping pincers, and show us how safe we were with him. But we five, his children, had dispersed across a continent, and rarely do we get together all at once, and never speak anymore of family outings. And so he studied the maps of the Atlas, wondering.

There were no crabs to be caught, no strong man to row us out. My boys had for their ocean the vast blue prairie sky, where the sun shone brilliantly, happy in its routine, a sky where northern lights danced at night. Sunday afternoons we would sit out front watching the cars displace the gulls on Main Street, churchgoers rolling by to worship, called by the bells that rang out so sweetly. Our dog beside us, smiling and panting, ears up, listening to the bells, tempted to sing along. Our home, this town, a sigh against the sky surrounded by endless horizon; where we'd sit, nearly in the middle of nowhere, on the century old stoop.

My boys would go fishing by the dam on the river sometimes bringing home jackfish and pickerel. The three of us would savour the abundance of buttery fish, feeding the leftovers to our excited dog. I would smile at my boys across our table, seeing in them the vitality of my father and my uncles, feeling a sense of connection, wondering if they had a sense of it themselves; wondering how they could, across so many miles. Perhaps they could cast across the cosmos — like a memory casts, like a fishing line casts — bridging worlds of land and water; cast toward generations, to family ties. From the upstairs of our house, we could look out across the prairie to see as far as we could see, unobstructed by buildings or hills, to where land became sky, to where one generation left off and the next started up, to where all things became issue from the hands of God.

God the Father, God the Son, and God the Holy Ghost. On Palm Sunday after church, my father would drive us to his mother's, where we'd eat Italian pastries and drink sweet vermouth. My grandmother set our gift, a blue hydrangea, by the window, smiling and admiring it, sighing, and murmuring in Italian. I had held the flower on my lap in the car, its blueness a sweet-smelling pillow against my face. I was glad my grandmother liked it as much as I did.

My father was her son. A trinity of sorts: she was his mother, he was her son, I, his prodigal daughter. He'd bring blessed palms from church so she could exchange them with us. It's a custom on Palm Sunday: the church blesses and distributes palms for people to exchange in commemoration of Christ's triumphant entry into Jerusalem. It must have been a great day for Christ. It was fun for us. Especially the burning of last year's palms, which had been kept the whole year; holy objects, hung in every room of our house, hung on walls by pictures of the Sacred Heart, or Mary, Mother of God, or tucked into the mirrors attached to dressers, to remind us to be holy ourselves.

The night before Palm Sunday, we'd gather all the palms from the previous year, and take them to my mother's kitchen to be burnt (you can never throw away something that's been blessed, you have to burn it). My mother would have the front burner of the gas stove turned up high, and one by one, she'd feed the palms to the flames. They burned quickly, dry as they were, and the aroma of them filled the house, a gorgeous, exotic, holy incense, that convinced us of their sacredness.

I gave my grandmother a palm and a kiss, wishing her a happy Palm Sunday, and she gave me a palm and kissed me, speaking on and on to me in Italian, her eyes searching mine meaningfully, as if I, her own granddaughter, must surely understand her, it being inconceivable to her that I would not. Her words were as mysterious to me as the Latin chanted at the Mass, a Eucharistic drink, heady, swirling, as sweet as the sweet vermouth, as fragrant as the blue hydrangea. To say that I have no idea what she said is not exactly true. It was important, and it made her sad, that much I know. And somehow I got the feeling it was about how she wished she could tell us more about Italy, the old country, and somehow it was about how she wanted us to remember her, to not forget her, and to pray, always, to the angels and saints for her, to ask them to help her because she was so lonely, she missed Italy so. I'm sure she missed Italy so.

My mother, Mary, was a different kind of grandmother to my boys. She got on a plane with my father, Dominick, and travelled to us, smiling, speaking accent-free English, wearing a special travel watch with two faces, one to tell the time back at her home, one to tell the time in ours. She and my father would come, she with her hair done, he in his suit, to sit in the backyard admiring the rabbits.

Later, my mother and I would cook, while my father inspected the house and yard for work he could busy himself with. He would go to the hardware store nearby and introduce himself, shaking the proprietor's hand and smiling warmly. My father loved hardware stores. He found great satisfaction in examining the paint brushes, flipping their bristles along the inside of his hand to select the softest one.

He painted the nine-foot high ceilings in the house white, always with a brush. He liked a brush, he would say, it does a better job. He always wanted to do a better job. A roller was easier — I should use a roller if I wanted to help him, it would be easier on me. But for him, always the brush, because it did a better job, and he was tough. He could paint a whole house with a brush, inside and out.

He would clean the brushes perfectly after each day's work, with Varsol, wetting the bristles and stroking them up and down the old newspapers he'd placed on the garage floor. Up and down, then back and forth he'd stroke, painting the newspaper with the leftover paint on his brush, pouring more Varsol on carefully to clean the brush thoroughly, turning each newspaper page when it had absorbed its limit, and continuing on, back and forth, up and down. Meticulously he worked, until the bristles shone like new. His brushes lasted a long time, but he painted our home a lot, buying new brushes often, good ones, searching the hardware store for them.

He bought us a wheelbarrow. No one could care for a house and yard without one. The garden tools, or the paint cans and brushes, or the bedding plants each spring, easily rolled to where they were needed. He would whistle, just as he did when he drove the car, rolling effortlessly. He rolled the wheelbarrow home from the hardware store full of tools: clippers, a hoe, a good hammer, paint and paint brushes. Rolled it into the yard of the house on Main Street like Santa with his sack of toys. My boys gave each other rides in the wheelbarrow, enjoying it as much as their grandfather did, emulating him as they worked by his side, imitating him long after he had left for home.

When he worked, he wore old clothes: old suit pants, old white shirts, old Florsheims. Never jeans, never sports shirts, never runners. No matter how much earth he dug in the garden, no matter how much he painted, he looked like a dignified man. My boys, striped T-shirts, shorts, runners, healthy and youthful, felt proud when they worked with their grandfather.

When I was growing up, he would stop in the stockroom to shine his shoes each morning before opening the store. I loved to watch this ceremony, the smell of the shoe polish as sweet as beeswax, the rhythm of the brushing which brought forth a shine, a crescendo, as exciting as any orchestrated by Beethoven. It was his ritual, reminding him of his roots as a shoe-shine boy in his father's shoe repair shop; and it was more, another attempt to beautify his world, to make an effort to do a better job. The black brush for his black shoes, the brown brush for his brown shoes, the shine they evoked a reflection of his relentless spirit.

The first time he was sick, the doctors said there was no hope. He would not believe them. He was fifty-five, hard working, clean living, successful; he deserved better. And from their black prediction that the cancer throughout his body would send him to an early grave, he turned, stubbornly fixing his will and energy, to a better future. He would not stop polishing his shoes each morning, he would not stop tending his yard and home. He fought, as he had rowed the rowboat, as if God had whispered in his ear. He fought with the same courage it took to reach for each menacing crab we hooked, reaching beyond the pincers to the place where he took hold and held tight. And because he did, he lived, and, many years later, could buy us a wheelbarrow, whistling as he rolled it to our home.

He'd build a fire for the barbecue. Crumpling newspapers one sheet at a time to make a deep bed for the briquettes. Shaking the briquettes carefully from the bag to form the fire bed. Lighting the paper here and there and there and there, like a cross. There was no escape for the briquettes; they would burn, cool black to white hot. He would place our food on the grill, the fat dripping down to the rising flames, sizzling. He would move the food away from high flames to cook more slowly, more deliciously, to keep the juiciness inside. My mother would pick the salad from the garden, wash it clean, splash it with virgin olive oil and red wine vinegar, and we would eat, astonished at the exquisiteness of such simplicity.

My father lived for decades after casting out the first cancer. That it came back at all relates somehow, I think, to the cycles that alternately bring good and evil into our lives. Something to do with the secrets of life and learning, of knowledge and trial. When he heard that he had to fight the cancer again, life had already worn down his body in many ways. His hearing diminished, he stooped in age where as a young man he'd stood tall, his black hair had thinned and silvered. But his sparkling eyes, his generous smile, his capable hands, remained, the brilliance of his spirit burnished by the goodness of his simple life.

The next time I drove past the house on Main Street, the roof was half off . Through it, the blue of the sky showed itself, shocking, entering where it never belonged. My youngest son's old bedroom now opened to the sky, leaving him unprotected from the night, from all the sky could hold. There was no escaping. If he were here, if we lived there, how would we hold back the sky?

The next time, the back wall was gone, erased, as if it never were. As if the decades had never been contained by this place in time.

The next time, the entire roof, gone and gone and gone. Upstairs, the window where my boys and I watched the Main Street parades, had been hauled away under the watchful eye of the gulls, the vault flung open to the swirling prairie wind. The happy youth of my boys, a whisper now.

I listen. The murmuring of my grandmother for her blue hydrangea. I listen. My father's easy whistling as he steers the wheelbarrow. I listen. My boys whispering to the rabbits not to fear. At night, the northern lights will come to dance in places where, when younger, we once dreamed. The planks, the boards, put into place so long ago, carried off, their final resting place unknown. The basement, newly filled with freshened earth.

I know some part of the earth's bright sunlight will forevermore be filtered through the coloured panes of stained glass from this house. My father's ancient finger traces a line across his Atlas, like the lines written on the palm of my hand. And I raise my eyes to his.

Son Of A Shoemaker

In pre-Gucci days, Italians called someone "a shoemaker" as an insult. My father's father was a shoemaker, but he was okay with that. He took pride in his work, he did a good job, a perfect job every time he turned his hand to anything. He wasn't ever sloppy, not in shoemaking, not in gardening, not in winemaking, not in cards. In fact, if he were alive today he would be going to a shrink for being such a fanatic about making things neat and beautiful. But back then, in the early 1900s, immigrants had to be fanatic to make the leaps required of them. There was no turning back, no round trip tickets. You either made it in a new world or died trying.

But my grandfather wasn't driven by fear of failure; he was driven by love of beauty. He loved beauty in everything, always he could see how to make a shoe, a plant, a grandchild, more beautiful with a shine, a rub, or a smile. My grandfather had self-respect even though he was a shoemaker because he knew what was going on inside his heart, he knew he was a good man. His friends knew that, too. They made wine together, grew gardens, smoked cigars, and played rummy day after day, year after year. They knew each other inside out. Anselmo and Jimmy, his lifelong friends whose children were lifelong friends as well. In those days, you inherited friends, and inherited enemies, too. Even inherited brides sometimes.

My grandfather's older brother, Nicolo, had fallen in love with Antonetta in the old country and sent for his bride-to-be: *cross the ocean and come marry me* he wrote on a penny post card. He had a job, a bright future, and they could start a life together in the New World. She did come over, Antonetta, young, small, beautiful, excited, in love with her husband-to-be, and ready to become his bride. She had embroidered her dress and petticoats, her camisoles, her hankies. We still have her clothing in our family, the dress she made for her wedding trip.

Nicolo and Antonetta would have married had tragedy not intervened. Nicolo was murdered, stabbed to death and gone in a cruel instant, leaving Antonetta alone in a strange land. After Nicolo's death, Antonetta was not a widow, not a bride-to-be, just a young, immigrant girl, crying for her lost love and her lost life. To return to Italy wasn't possible. No one ever went home without shame. Besides, she was penniless and the penniless couldn't buy passage. That was when my grandfather the shoemaker, Pasquale, did the right thing.

As was the custom in the Old World, he himself married Antonetta, my grandmother, his brother's one true love. It saved her life. She didn't have to return to Italy shamed at her bad luck. She didn't have to face what the villagers would see as her foolishness in forsaking Italy for a man who was stupid enough to leave home and go where he could be murdered. She didn't have to stay as a stranger in the New World working, if she were lucky, in a factory. She didn't have to consider other shameful, sinful, work. She married my grandfather and they had three sons; my father was the middle child.

My father, Dominick, loved his mother and emulated Pop, his father. His first job was as a shoeshine boy in his father's shoe repair, applying polish to shoes and brushing them until they gleamed. Throughout his life, he followed his father's example:

he took pride in everything he did in life because he always did his best, from his rose gardens, to his fig grove, to his children's education, to his home and family.

Shining shoes became a symbol of how he led his life. He shined his own shoes daily in the morning before opening the store we lived over. He kept his shoeshine box in the storeroom and stopped there before 9 AM, in time to put the brown polish on the brown shoes, or the black polish on the black shoes, letting the polish dry, then taking the brush that matched brown to brown, black to black. He stroked this way then that, the front, sides, and back of each shoe, so that the leather smiled back at him when he examined it. Every day, no matter how sick he was — and for many years he fought, and beat, and fought, and beat, cancer — every day, no matter how upside down the world was turning, with his children's troubles, and the evaporation of the plans he had made for his own life, every day he shined his shoes. With each stroke he coaxed them from dullness into brightness. And each and every day of his life was started with this ritual.

His father and mother, after thirty years, lived apart. I can only guess, but probably the first love in a young woman's life never dies, even if he does. My grandmother, I'm sure, tried hard to lay Nicolo to rest, and to love my grandfather instead. My grandfather, I'm sure, tried to love my grandmother, even though her heart lay elsewhere. My father, I'm sure, loved them both, and did what he could to honour them.

On Mother's Day we visited Grandma, on Father's Day we visited Grandpa, and those days and every other day in between, my father shined his shoes. They say that the flap of a butterfly's wings across the globe affects the winds all over the world. I wonder about that and about the shoe-shining ritual whenever I think about my grandfather's death. I wonder how, after decades of being angry in a house apart from his wife, he returned to her to die, returned to the bed he had chosen as a young man, with the wife he had chosen because it was the right thing to do. Returned to where the shoe repair downstairs had been his shop, the place where his boys had learned to shine shoes, and where my father learned to live life by bringing a shine to every moment of every day.

When my Grandfather died, he was the first of our family to go, leaving behind his friends, Anselmo and Jimmy, his wife, Antonetta, his three sons, their wives, and us, his grandchildren. He must have been frightened to go alone after crossing oceans and planting gardens always with friends and family. But I'm sure his murdered brother, Nicolo, greeted him on the other side, if only to say what my grandfather knew in his heart, that he was a good man, well-meaning, who, all things considered, had done his best to bring order and beauty into the world. And had produced my father, whose simplicity and steadfastness had shone a light home.

Customs

As far back as I can remember, we would drive down on a Sunday afternoon from our home in northern New Jersey, to Fairhaven, to where my grandfather lived, alone, in a house guarded by two stone lions. The lions were watchful as we pulled into Grandpa's long black driveway all the way to the back of the house, where Grandpa stood on the porch, waving and smiling at us.

After a toast of his homemade wine, and games of pinochle played on the green Formica table in his kitchen, we children emerged from shrouds of Grandpa's cigar smoke out onto the green, sunny, front lawn to feed the stone lions berries from the bushes nearby. Placing each berry gingerly inside their opened jaws, next to the bulbs which illuminated their fierce faces at night, we sensed the lions' awareness that they were receiving a most treasured offering. Just as we recognized the sacredness of the pure white host of Holy Communion, they knew the berries to be a secret, sacred fruit, shared only with those most loyal, most trusted by our family. The lions fed, we would then go out back to Grandpa's garden to pick the salad for our supper.

Inside the kitchen, my mother would start the macaroni water, its steam rising starchy and straight from the huge pot up into the dark, pungent clouds of grandpa's cigar smoke. She would stand next to the stove near the pot, watching, guarding, waiting, like the lions. Grandpa smoked. My mother cooked. Their vapours battled in the air.

My father would sit by Grandpa, watching the baseball game on television with him. They would comment on the good players, or on the crowd, or on the weather. Or if there was nothing on the television to watch, they would talk about Fairhaven, about the firehouse next door, about the new restaurant on the river, about Grandpa's shoe repair shop. There was a familiarity between them, the father and son, a shared history, an understanding. And because of this, they would not talk about why Grandpa had moved out of Grandma's house. Or how he managed alone, with no one to cook macaroni for him. Because they were so close, they never spoke of it. It was a silent pact between them.

In the garden, flecks of the rich black soil clung to Grandpa's ripe warm tomatoes. My sisters and I brushed them off and bit into flesh so tasty our eyes would shut tight with pleasure. From the kitchen window, our mother would call to us to wash them first, but we were far enough away to not hear so well, the dusty soil part of the exquisite taste we loved. Tomatoes and lettuce we gathered in the sloop of our shirts; scallions we made into whistles, piping happy songs into their reeds until they split. Brushing through the lush rows of tomato plants, we inspected the onions, the garlic, the zucchini, and the peppers, choosing some of each for the enormous salad.

Until Grandpa died and the house was sold, that garden grew, those lions watched.

My father had grown only roses in our backyard — beautiful roses, but still, only roses. But after Grandpa died, my father dug a garden, a memorial garden. It grew easily, luxuriant and prolific, as if Grandpa had enlisted all the angels in Heaven to look after it. Then, quietly and without ceremony, my father escorted the first fig tree into our backyard. A humble, skinny tree, it rooted timidly, and grew weakly at first, even though wrapped for winter and coddled through summer. Hesitant, yet sturdy, an undeniable earthiness radiated in its delicacy. Grandpa had not grown figs; it was a novelty.

My father tended that first frail tree as if it were his child, his own flesh and blood. He would work in the garden, as one might imagine Jehovah working in *his* garden; tending with love and great expectations this fig tree, this little bit of nothing, this scrawny and trembling scrap of imagined grandeur. He toiled as he must have seen his father toil, bending, and digging, sweating in the warm golden sun. Winters were too harsh; summers were too dry; but my father's heart was constant in its caring, and after a while, the first figs appeared — as miraculous an apparition as ever appeared to a Roman. Small and green, five in number — few for an entire year's crop but the very essence of sweetness and succulence.

By the following year, the figs had multiplied like the loaves and fishes. The starlings had heard about the figs. Figs went missing, stolen in the earliest light, dropped half-eaten in the starlings' haste to escape. At the window my father would spot the thieves in the morning mist. He would chase them, waving the straw broom high overhead, entreating Heaven and all the angels and saints to see what the starlings had done to his figs.

He made a net to protect his tree then, the starlings sent away hungry, cursing across the sky. The next year brought another heavenly harvest of figs. And the following year, a second tree was planted, tended, and defended; its fruit sweet enough for angels. In following years, another tree, and yet another were planted, each cared for with the same diligence, until there grew a lovely grove of gentle, verdant fig trees. The garden continued to flourish, too, and my father brought my mother armfuls of vegetables, bowls of figs, and blood-red roses, and she sat in his lap and kissed him, delighted.

As time moved on, the fig trees grew taller and stronger, but my parents grew smaller and softer. Macaroni still cooked, though more slowly, and ripe figs still appeared each dawn in summer, though a bowlful took longer to gather, and felt heavier in the crook of my father's arm. We children moved away, leaving the afternoon sunshine to fall in silence across their living room floor.

Now I visit with the excitement of old, knowing that my father's figs will reawaken a cornucopia of memories: of Grandpa's garden, of incomparable salads splashed with virgin olive oil and homemade red wine vinegar, of the warm summer sunshine seducing the sweet, sweet earth in a ritual which runs thick through our family's peasant blood.

All the children and grandchildren come, by car and plane, across borders of every kind. Passports are shown, declarations made at Customs. We bring with us spouses whose grandfathers drank vodka and whiskey, not red wine. Whose mothers tended perogies or potatoes, not macaroni. Whose fathers played poker and watched football rather than planted fig trees.

When we sisters gather together in the kitchen to cook, we love to share memories of the old days. If our mother hears us, she is always surprised at how much we remember about those times. And at the supper table, when our father serves fresh figs for desert, he fields our questions which arise out of every bite; questions not about raising excellent figs, as one might expect, but about a different era: the old days, days of shops and gardens and oceans teaming with relatives in search of a new home. Of names changed from Pasquale to Paul, from Orellio to Jimmy. This pleases him, as if the figs were a key, opening a door to a room seldom used, a room full of treasures he was saving especially for us.

During these gatherings, peace reigns; quarrels, set aside. Our growing up together had never been like this, but you would think it had, abundant with tolerance, deference, and understanding. Now, we come to listen, not to talk; to hear stories — their stories. Our stories. The grandchildren think the world has changed since we were young, for this peace is unknown to them outside this small precious time and space.

One Sunday morning after Mass, after my father has picked us fresh figs for breakfast and my mother has brewed a pot of coffee, a question I have never considered comes to my mind, and aloud I ask, "Why grow figs? Grandpa didn't grow figs, did he?" And my father shrugs so slightly he seems almost shy, the answer coming not from that part of him which carefully recounts the details of our ever fading family history, not from that part of him which delights in relating details of quaint Italian custom; but the answer coming from a son's simple ever-loving heart, "My mother loved figs." Then a silence fell upon us all, like the silence at the Consecration, and we understood what had been revealed. It was his way to reunite his parents, to plant the garden for his father, and the figs for his mother. The abundant harvest of the two a sign to him that they were happy together in Heaven, their differences set to rest for all time.

Saying goodbye takes forever. Promises to take care, to watch out, to keep in touch. Then for each household, a small box of figs to take home, each fig wrapped in soft paper to prevent bruising, each bearing the thumbprint of the family. One box goes west, another south, still another comes with me through customs at the airport.

"Are you taking any fresh produce?" a questionnaire demands authoritatively. "What is the value of the goods you are taking out of the country?" The customs agents are in uniform and the rules laid out clearly. I feel a surge like blood from a fresh, deep wound. I quickly check the box of figs in my carry-on, and see it is secure. I wonder if priests declare the Viaticum. And then the magic dust of memory quells my fear, and the feeling I have is as the stone lions who guarded my grandfather's home must have felt, their fierce open jaws full of the holy berries, their timeless vigilance ever constant.

Famous In the Middle Of Nowhere

An explanation to my father on his death

My father's funeral brought us together in incense, candlelight, memory, and hope. His name was Dominick. I was, I am, his daughter.

I had moved far away from him, across a continent, to a different country, confounding and frustrating his old world expectations that I would stay close to him, near enough so that he could care for me, know me, all my life. I had raised my sons, his pall bearers, on the Canadian prairie, away from the beloved home above his store in New Jersey where I had grown up. Only weeks before his death, he had pleaded my return, offering a home, and the company of my sisters who had remained there with him.

The distance which had separated us dissolves, and I feel his strong hand on my shoulder, hear his voice in my ear: are you listening? Here I am. *I stand miniscule against the prairie horizon, the wind whipping me in gusts. An eagle swoops, its talons grip the back of my shirt and up into the swirling blue sky I soar.*

Long distance . . . on Father's Day. Christmas Day. Labour Day. Valentine's Day. Long distance. Easter Sunday. Each birthday. Happy birthday. The strong prairie wind blowing. Thirty below zero. Forty below. Happy Birthday, baby. 425 Jackson Avenue was the springboard for his hopes and dreams. There, he shined shoes in his father's shoe repair shop, dutifully, deliberately. With each stroke of the brush, he practiced creating the exquisite shine that would permeate his long life. With a gentle, skillful hand, he stroked every shoe as he did each day of his life, to a blindingly brilliant gleam.

I loved to watch as he worked in the fig orchard, his aging face kind and patient, eyes bright as his hand inspected one young fig tree, then the next. Their beauty delighted him in a profound way, as if they connected him to an orchard in Italy, where a man just like him shared his love of the figs, the two united by a rainbow arching clear across the globe. In the fall, he wrapped his fig trees in leaves and burlap, bundled against the awful howls of winter. He wanted me in his orchard as well, to be wrapped in the comfort of his warmth, connected to our kin in Italy.

I thrill in facing the prairie's winter wind head on, let it burn and bite my brightened cheeks; thrill as well to the hot burning sun of summer; live without shade on the fiery prairie. Who would guess, on the peaceful summer prairie, as songbirds sing and swallows swoop, that in the wind I would hear my name.

My father came to visit me at university, picking me up in his station wagon to buy me fruit at the Italian market. He shopped with me, selecting apples with thick, deep red skins, collecting the most ripe aromatic pears, and handfuls of luscious purple and green grapes. His visit puzzled me, all this distance to buy me fruit; puzzled me until I opened the door to leave his car, my arms laden with his gifts. Then he spoke, his concern for me, my need for the sweetness of fruit, and all at once I understood, understood what each of Dominick's daughters eventually understood, that his dream for each of us was for a sweet life. He sensed something was wrong in my world, something he would prune away if he could. And if he couldn't, his heart would break.

❦ ❦ ❦

I BROUGHT MY FIRST SON, A CHILD born with his grandfather's same protective spirit, brought him, to this wide prairie landscape. So like his grandfather, he brought me dandelions in shady sunlight, kissed my cheek and smiled into my eyes. His solid spirit never bent by the winds, he calmed my fiery soul with his sweetness. For love of him my eyes would quit their search of the horizon.

In the summers of my girlhood, my father would take us to the Jersey shore, our cottage surrounded by his rose beds, the salt air keen against the delicate blooms. He would work in early mornings before the day heated and grew harsh, before the day could shake itself full awake he would trim, hoe, water, lifting the head of one bloom after the other, murmuring in Italian. Wherever he turned his hand, there grew exquisite beauty.

His garden, too, rows of proud tomatoes, scallions, near-black eggplant, shining, sweet, abundant. His Florsheims padded across the soil, well-shined still and not forgotten despite their age, he moved in where the rows allowed him, reaching down and pulling weeds, picking the ripened vegetables for supper, smiling at the new ones coming, turning them to bathe in sunlight, to grow in sunlight.

At his wake, my mother said her last farewell, cradling my father's face in her soft hands, how handsome he was she said over and over. How handsome. She kissed him, her soft lips on his cold cheek, her hand stroking across his brow, a brow untroubled now by pain, kissed him and softly murmured to him.

At his funeral Mass we gave thanks for his good life, just as he had given thanks for our good life every Thanksgiving at our home. Year after year as we grew up, the scene had been the same: the family seated around the dining room table, he at the head saying grace. The luscious roast turkey, stuffed, scrumptious, and steaming, arrived at the table on a platter presented by my mother. She had cooked the turkey, now he would carve it, a task he did very painstakingly.

My father sliced, then laid each piece on the serving platter. Perfect slices of white meat, neatly severed chunks of dark meat, arranged in orderly rows, enough to give each of us the kind we wanted and more. I could have grasped a drumstick in my hands, its hot flesh burning mine, fat and juices running down my chin as I bit down in satisfaction, crazy with desire. To him, Thanksgiving meant waiting, savouring, appreciating, sharing — something I needed to learn. In winter, we children would come from school into the warm steamy air of my father's store, our cheeks and fingers frozen, walking around behind the counter and past our father on our journey to our home upstairs. One memory so unforgettable, his store quiet and empty, I return from school alone, my sisters and brother elsewhere, the day particularly bitter with cold. My father, seated on the steps to his office, taking my small cold hands in his large warm ones, and placing them, first the one, then the other, under his armpits to warm. His eyes, level with mine, looking sadly sweet as he explained, "My mother used to do this to warm our hands in winter." For a time we stayed in that position, the heat of his body gently warming me, delicately, this earthy gesture a sweet and sacred moment, his eyes level with mine, recalling his own mother's warming love.

The steering wheel, in forty degree below weather, so desperately cold no gloves can hold it, no heater touch its core. Even in thick, heavy boots, my toes freeze. The road disappears, snow covered and flat as the surrounding prairie. I drive by instinct, wondering why I left the safety of my father's warming ways. My children have made friends with this cold, finding warmth where I find only chill, and in their smiles and hardiness

I seek more sacred warmth, seeing there my father's eyes, and circles of memory.

The sun dogs, clustered crystal rainbows, gleam on either side of the sun, a sign the air has moved to another state of being, shining, waiting, watching. Blindingly brilliant, beautiful, a special gift in this glacial place, the sun dogs surprise sky watchers, a call to remember warmth and peace in the middle of what is neither warm nor peaceful, in the middle of winter's icy smack.

My cancer came in a deadly silent moment. No music blaring, no howling wind, just one cold finger, quiet on my breast. A note, so rare, from my father, telling of how he remembered me at my birth, remembered my first communion, remembered me as a girl; as if in remembering me his memories could hold me in life, connect me to him, to this world. And they did. He cradled my face in his large, strong hands, and smiled, his sparkling eyes saying, "Here, look here, not there, look here. See? Only love . . . see only love . . ."

It was January when my father died, I left the forty-five degree below zero temperatures on the prairie to process behind his coffin into the church in New Jersey, that coffin borne by old friends and my two sons. In the warmth of the vigil lights on the altar were my father's countless prayers for me, his smiles for me, his looks of love as he tirelessly and daily coaxed me to a gleam dreamed within his patient yet insistent heart. I would not be dulled, he would not allow it, not while he was on this earth, nor now, even when beyond. In his world, the beautiful came forth from the mud, withstood the winters; under his hand, roses, and figs, and humble shoes shone like suns.

Long distance through the phone lines to my mother, we both expect to hear him there, asking about the weather, wishing me Happy Birthday.

We pause where in the past he would have spoken, waiting to hear his voice, missing him.

The prairie wind is different to me now, filtered through the whispered call I hear. The voice of Dominick, more than father now, part of all that sees me on the plains, sees me yearning for the spirit wind. A butterfly, a cloud, a seed borne by the breezes, putting up his hand against the wind to shelter me, his arm around my shoulders against the cold as I walk in winter.

My father always wanted to be with me. How like him to persist along the horizon, across this giant sky; his tenderness, his sparkling eyes, in sky and snow and sunlight, gentling the howl of the abiding wind.

Food For the Funeral

A FUNERAL MAKES EVERYBODY HUNGRY; IT'S A paradox like, "The King is dead, Long live the King! Let's eat!" And the more funerals you go to the more you need to eat something. For Pop, we'll have the usual, of course, sandwiches cut in triangles and squares, egg salad, ham salad, salmon salad, cheese, two kinds of pickles, potato salad, three bean salad, matrimonial cake and butter tarts. The ones on a diet will need something like a green salad with low calorie dressing or they won't be happy. Nobody on a diet is happy. Why do they diet if it makes them unhappy? Everybody should eat and be happy — especially at a funeral.

And then the coffee. Everybody will want coffee, and tea, and the young people will want Coca-Cola. Is Dr. Pepper okay at a funeral, or is that going too far?

As for the vegetarians, who knows what they'll drink or eat, maybe carrots and celery, a raw vegetable tray with a sour cream dip. God help them, their insides must get tired of grinding raw vegetables. And we'll have radishes cut like roses. Pop loved roses. What's nice is green bean vinaigrette, artichoke hearts, marinated mushrooms, Pop loved those, so we'll have them too.

And cheeses, cheddar and gouda, and what about provologne, mozzarella, Asiago, Pop would have liked that, the beautiful cheeses, he had a thing for good cheese, blue cheese, Brie,

Camembert, goat cheese. Watch Cousin Rocky around the cheeses though, he must have been a mouse in a former life.

And chocolate, let's have lots of chocolates in Pop's memory — nut clusters, pecans, walnuts, chocolate-covered cashews, everybody will want those, too; Rocky alone will eat a dozen.

And some salami — Genoa, and Calibrese, and some prosciutto, capicola, bresaola, mortadella.

And olives of course, the black with garlic, and the green, the ones they make special in the deli, you have to have olives, the brown, the black, the green, the big, the little, the smooth, the wrinkled; the olives, they look like us, the family, yes? Lots of olives.

And good Italian bread with a nice crust from Giogio's, and some red wine, we won't get enough in church, red wine and white, too, for the ones who get a headache from the red, and some Campari, for the *agitato*.

Maybe a nice baked ham for sandwiches, and Aunt Josie's meatballs, some Italian sausage. Pop would want sausage, and red peppers with garlic, and oil like Mom used to make at home all the time — he would want that.

And roasted chestnuts, almonds, hazelnuts like Alberto grows in Conca, you have to have nuts, and fruit, he'd want fruit, green grapes, red grapes, pears — they have to be ripe — and his figs, of course, from his trees, how could we have a funeral for him without his figs?

And the pastries, everybody likes the pastries, Rocky alone will eat every one if we don't watch him, we'll have to guard the cannoli for sure. Pop always liked the sfogliatelle best, and the cookies, the ones with the ends dipped in chocolate, and he loved the pinola cookies, too, loved them, and the pinched Amaretti, and the lemon half-moons.

We want it to be nice for him, all his favourites, lots of them, lots extra so he can take some home with him, just in case it's the last time he tastes them, God forbid, just in case Heaven is catered by McDonald's. That would be a shock, wouldn't it, seeing Ronald McDonald standing next to Saint Peter at the Pearly Gates? How can you live in Eternity without good Italian food? Pop would die if we sent him to Heaven without good Italian food. He would die for good. Let's get extra wine. Let's get the best Italian bread. Let's have all the best for him.

All the best. You only die once.

MOTHER MARY

Mama's Purse

My mother, a fashionable woman of her time, prided herself on the abundance of purses in her wardrobe. She had straw summer purses with plastic fruits on the front, she had fall purses decorated with tapestries of autumn leaves, leather purses edged in Florentine gold, Easter purses with embroidered bunnies and chicks, purses with large flowers, small flowers, red cardinals, fish; beaded purses, ship-shaped purses for sailing — you name it, she had it.

Always large, roomy purses to carry many, many, many things. My father once weighed one of my mother's purses — thirty-five pounds. No kidding. My mother's purses were not merely beautiful, they were functional. And magical. She carried everything imaginable — and often things beyond imagination — in her purses.

When we'd go on a trip in our family's pale blue Packard, my parents and us five kids, we'd play games to pass the time. We'd count red cars, blue ones, or white; we'd sing *Row Row Row Your Boat*; we'd play games like I Spy, Twenty Questions. We'd look out the car window at cows and crops and small towns along the way, the world running by like a flickering film — abandoned cars in fields, a horse behind a fence, clotheslines full of coloured shirts and rows of underwear.

After a while, we kids would fidget, wanting to stop for food or gift shops, something, anything. My father, a man who enjoyed being somewhere more than getting somewhere, was loath to do that. So, my mother, in those moments of early discord, would open her purse and draw out some treats for us.

An orange would emerge, and a banana. The nails on her long elegant fingers always polished with red would vanish into the mysterious depths of her purse over and over again, this time retrieving a napkin to spread on her lap to protect her dress, then a knife to cut the fruit she peeled and sectioned so delicately for her children and her husband. A bottle of sarsaparilla soda and seven of the tiniest paper Dixie cups, poured half full so as not to spill in the car; then cheese that she'd slice with the fruit knife; then crackers; then chocolate coins wrapped in golden foil, or Hershey's candy Kisses, or Tootsie Rolls. Her purse was a treasure chest, bottomless, wondrous. Her hand would disappear and search, while we children watched with as much anticipation as if she were a magician reaching into a top hat to pull out a soft, wiggly rabbit.

And it wasn't just food. Maps, toys, plastic rain hats, tissues, earrings, rosary beads, mantillas, a bottle of Holy Water, artificial flower corsages, a sewing kit, *everything*. As the years went on, she continued to surprise us with what was in there. When my eldest sister started university, my parents and us five kids all travelled with her and her suitcases to the school dorm that would be her home for the next four years. A small bottle of red wine and seven plastic wine glasses emerged to help us celebrate the occasion, my mother pulling them from her purse with a flourish one after the other after the other to our utter delight. It was almost as if the Holy Water and rosaries she carried in there were working miracles, providing her with a direct chute to Heaven's supply depot.

And as we, her four daughters grew, our own simple purses ever at our sides, there would be other, more serious, car rides — like the funeral corteges that came all at once the winter I was thirteen. Two grandmothers and a grandfather, all dying within a month of each other, as if there was a discount rate offered for groups and the three of them had decided to take a little trip together, a family journey, if not to Italy, then the next best thing, a trip to Heaven. It was very Italian, which we were. And very Catholic, which we also were.

There were three days of wakes for each grandparent. Streams of relatives sad and weeping, cousins congregating to pray with sorrowful faces, everyone dressed for death in funereal black. We besieged Heaven with our prayers for the souls of the dearly departed.

For Grandma Michelina, whose rosary beads had worn grooves in her fingertips from constant use. Pray for her.

For Grandpa Pasquale, who had gardened and played pinochle. Pray for him.

For Grandma Antonetta, who always stood at the window, waiting for visitors. Pray for her.

Bless these and all the dearly departed, we prayed and prayed and prayed.

Who knows why we thought these three needed so many prayers. Maybe they were wild in their youth.

We hadn't expected any of them to die, much less one after the other after the other. It was very operatic, and everyone took it in stride, weeping and praying while dressed in nice black clothing.

The open caskets with their quilted pillows looked so very comfortable, as if Michelina, Pasquale, and Antonetta were only sleeping, and it comforted us to think they were asleep and dreaming, not dead, never to return. We whispered quietly so as not to disturb them during each three-day wake. We had been trained to be quiet in Church, and the quietness surrounding our sleeping grandparents felt-right to us, holy, as holy as Heaven. Unlike the Irish, as I would later learn from my Irish husband's family, who believed those left behind must try their very best to wake the departed from their eternal rest (this, I believe, was because none of his family ever expected to get to Heaven). But not so with my family where everyone believed a corpse should be allowed to sleep right through a wake undisturbed. Different viewpoints, but the end result was the same — a burial.

First, a fine funeral mass in the old Latin rite was said — one for Michelina, one for Pasquale, one for Antonetta. High Masses, all of them, with candles everywhere, thick incense rising to Heaven carrying our prayers. But even though we were good Italians, regularly attending Masses for the living as well as the dead, the solemnity of it all wore thin by the third funeral, and, well, we four girls all being teenagers and not that practiced at either marathon-length reverence or the finer points of funereal behaviour, eventually felt challenged to be so somber.

We rode in the funeral parlour's limousines time after time after time, reflective the first time, accustomed the second, downright giddy by the third, knowing the routine, and kind of unnerved by this death craze. We wished we could be anywhere with our friends instead of at yet another post-cemetery breakfast for the dead.

Our mother expected no better behaviour from us, understanding that the young can only take so much in the way of funerals, and so, in her purse, she carried hard candies from Paris, which she passed out in the limousine en route to the graveyard. She offered us her new colours of lipstick which gave us something different to do in the limo and which kept us focused on the appearance of propriety. We got through those funerals, and others after them, our mother and her purse a magical resource throughout.

As we grew older and had families of our own, our cars would travel together in caravans, children in tow, our coolers full of drinks, economy sized bags of potato chips and pretzels from the 7 Eleven. Wherever we landed, my mother would wow us with something from her purse — figs from my father's orchard, a bottle of Cherry Liquor, souvenirs from Italy — we never knew what she'd have in there. And if we went to church with her, she'd dig down and find mantillas for us all, to cover our heads in lacy loveliness, so that we'd feel as special and wonderful as the veiled statue of Mary, the Mother of God.

All four or us had married, and all four married non-Italians. Some, like me, married Irishmen, some Germans, some both. We got married an awful lot, actually, more than good Catholics are supposed to. My sister, Carol, moved to Pennsylvania, got married twice, the second time to Jerry, a Ukrainian ten years her senior.

Now that's an interesting mix, Italians and Ukrainians; never a lack of food at those gatherings. Carol and her Ukrainians lived in Pennsylvania, less than two hours from my mother, who lived in New Jersey. The visiting back and forth was frequent and fun, and Carol's Ukrainian sister-in-law, Lydia, although in many ways the opposite of my mother, became her friend.

Lydia was a free-spirit, totally unconcerned with the opinions of other people. She could not care less if her purse matched her shoes. But she liked to make people happy, she liked to feed them, and she liked to compliment them so that she could see them smile. And if they smiled, she couldn't help but love them. And if you complimented my mother, she couldn't help but love you. So, all in all, Lydia and my mother got along famously.

Of course they both were big on the church. Not that they were serious about religion so much as they loved the fancy clothes that the priests wore, and the holiness of the services, the beautiful church buildings, the angels and saints who lived with God in Heaven. My mother, of the Roman rite, loved the stained glass windows. Lydia, of the Ukrainian Orthodox rite, loved the icons. As for all the rules and Thou Shalt Nots, well, they were both accomplished women who had raised many children, women whose households shone with spotlessness. Who was going to tell them what the rules were?

Nobody, that's who. And so it came to pass that Lydia, good Ukrainian Orthodox lady that she was, decided that when her time came, she didn't want to be buried in the ground, she wanted to be cremated. Now her church didn't allow cremation. But did that matter? Her eyebrows arched and her neck stretched tall as a crane's when she told the great lot of us gathered for Christmas Eve supper around her table, a table so long it filled two rooms of her house and then some, that she wasn't going into the dirt, she had cleaned and cleaned her whole life and she wasn't about to spend Eternity in dirt thank you very much, she was going into the fire to be cremated and that was that. Her wishes were clear. Everyone knew, and she promised to haunt anyone who argued with her about it. The matter was dropped.

Dropped until Lydia dropped, some years later. My mother took it hard. But she had seen so many go: my dad, her brother Alberto, her sister Josie, so very many others, nearly everyone she ever knew. Her funeral blacks fresh from the cleaners, sadly but resignedly she got ready to go to the services for Lydia.

Meanwhile, remembering Lydia's wish, my sister, Carol, and her husband, Jerry, quietly had Lydia cremated. It had to be done privately, since the church didn't approve, and no one wanted Heaven to be alerted to Lydia's last renegade activity. Her ashes collected into a graceful urn, Carol and Jerry took Lydia home with them to await the gathering of friends and family for the services of farewell at church.

We drove through the sunny Pennsylvanian countryside to get to the tiny old Ukrainian church where the wake and service for Lydia were to be held. I travelled with my mother, driving for her. In the two-hour trip, we went from the thick of the city to the forest and small towns where Lydia had lived. Leaves of the trees, amber and gold, reminded my mother of the countryside she had loved as a girl. She looked so dignified in her fine black suit and long cloth coat, the handles of an enormous black leather purse over her arm. A surge of emotion flushed me with warmth, and tears suddenly filled my eyes and spilled over my cheeks. I realized someday, someday soon perhaps, it would be her funeral I was attending. Her hand reached across to squeeze my arm, as if she knew my thoughts, and she sighed softly. Reaching into her purse, she drew out a manila envelope. "I want a closed casket. With this picture in a frame. I don't want anyone seeing me dead." Mom slipped the envelope onto the seat between us, and I reached across to squeeze her hand, the rest of the journey spent in silence, our hands holding onto each other through sighs and bittersweet smiles.

At the Ukrainian church, Carol and Jerry held Lydia's urn as they spoke earnestly to the priest. There was a problem. My other sisters filled us in: no urns, no ashes allowed in the church. Lydia would not be allowed to attend her own funeral.

My mother drew herself up to her full five feet of height and, with gracefulness and a subtle steely determination, walked across to Carol, Jerry, Lydia in the urn, and the priest, while we, her daughters, followed behind like well behaved goslings.

Her head held high with dignity, my mother greeted the priest respectfully, warmly touched my sister's arm, then Jerry's, then with the thumb of her gloved right hand traced a cross on Lydia's urn. The priest tried not to notice. The wave of sadness that passed through her in seeing her friend overwhelmed her, and I steadied her as she wept. Even the priest was touched by her grief. She sighed ever so deeply, as if her sigh could help propel Lydia on to Heaven, then a calm seemed to overtake her.

"Lydia was such a wonderful woman. Did you know her, Father?"

"A wonderful woman. Yes, I knew her well."

"Eight children! And such a *good* woman!" my mother went on.

"She is with us in spirit," the priest said predictably.

My mother reached again to the urn and made the sign of the cross in blessing. "Her last day with us."

The priest looked at his watch. "We need to start the services."

"Father," Jerry pleaded, "she doesn't have to be on the altar — off to the side somewhere. You won't even know she's there."

"I'm sorry, it's just impossible," the priest replied firmly. "The church is very strict about this. No cremation, no ashes allowed in the church. It was her decision and she understood the rules. We can have a memorial service, but no Mass, and her ashes — well, may she rest in peace. You understand my situation? The rest of the church community has to know that the church is serious about what it teaches."

"We'll put one of those cloths over her, like you put on the tabernacles!" Jerry pleaded.

The priest pressed his fingertips against his brow. I think he had a headache. My mother laid her hand on Jerry's arm to quiet him. "It's all right, Jerry. Lydia would understand." Turning to the priest she said warmly, "Thank you, Father."

Visibly relieved, the priest vanished into the sanctuary of the church, leaving us all despondent. Carol and Jerry looked to each other, in dread of having to tell the rest of the family of the priest's decision and leave Lydia out in the car while we went inside for her funeral. My mother looked at Carol, then Jerry, then quietly indicated for us to come close to her, to come closer and closer.

"Here," she said to Carol, who was holding the urn, "give her to me." And with that she took Lydia's ashes and carefully slipped them into her large purse, making us all smile in astonishment. Carol helped her draw the zipper across the top of her purse, hiding Lydia's urn completely from view. "She can come with me."

The priest chanted, the incense rose, the candles stretched and stretched towards Heaven. The priest did everything in his power to ease Lydia's journey to the other world. But he was merely a man, and though his vestments were of finest silk and satin, and even though his forehead had been anointed with the sacrament of Holy Orders, there were some powers which eluded him, powers which women like my mother would forever hold in graceful palms, wrapped in embroidered hankies, guarded by mysterious smiles.

We daughters went through my mother's purses eventually, dividing them, assigning them, selecting them. The magic wasn't there, of course, but no surprise. It is an inner grace to see what miracles might be wrought from little things like loaves and fishes. An inner grace to pack a lunch, a purse, a suitcase, with foreknowledge. An inner grace to see where God steps back and mothers take over. Of the many secrets to be learned upon the earth, some of the very best are infinitesimal and never noticed. And like a shaft of light direct from the heavens, we sometimes glow with the magic we have found in long-forgotten pockets, and long-remembered moments when, behind God's back, we have glimpsed the glorious.

CROSSING THE PACIFIC

To My Mother

I CROSSED THE PACIFIC BY PLANE TO meet my daughter-in-law's family in Japan seventy-one years after you crossed the fierce Atlantic at eye level, you and Grandma and the rest. Oceans were bigger then, you may as well have swum your journey took so long.

The Pacific never touched me in my crossing. Like an angel, sanctified and holy, I flew above it. No salt burned my cheek or my tongue. No fearful prayer petitioned Heaven — I was already in the heavens at 37,000 feet competing with God Himself for elbow room.

But you, you left the sheep in the olive grove, you left the restful sloping hillsides of Italy to set out onto water so terrifying Jesus Himself would not have walked on it — the dark and endless Atlantic surely the cauldron of every witch and devil exiled from goodness and God.

Our ancestors had lived in Italy from forever to that day of your departure. There in the village, graves and caves and volcanoes could swallow you up, but they were nothing compared to this Hell of the Atlantic's water, this changeling water, water in unimaginable abundance yet unfit to drink. Unfit to bless.

Surely the waters of home called to you during this crossing: the well in your village, the river where you washed clothes on the rocks, the baptismal font where the Gates of Heaven opened to you with purity, with prayer, with Holy Water. Who would have thought another of water's faces could ever be as profane as this Atlantic Ocean.

I, too, have crossed oceans in my life, times of change, times of trial, walking new paths, but nothing compared to this ocean crossing of yours.

Yours was the age of innocence, when the world was enormous and unscientific, when we humans were insignificant, confined to villages just like Conca — the one you left. Lives were local back then, filled with mysteries, rituals, and ancient wisdom to protect us from the underworld, the unexplored, and the unknown realms where daemons reigned.

In swallowing your fear and stepping aboard that ship, you cupped the ocean, scooped it into the sloop of your skirt, mapped it, named it, made it memory in our family history, so that I, as your daughter, came to earth a descendent of one who had faced and conquered the earth's mightiest waters.

After your extraordinary bravery in doing that, for me to fly in a Boeing across the sweet Pacific to meet Japanese relatives was purely ceremonial.

Untying Knots

THE BAKERS TIED EVERY BOX WITH STRING from a tall ball on a peg, knotting shut each boxful of cookies, each coffee cake, each long, low box of éclairs secure in its own cardboard space. If many treats went to the same lucky place then the string would whip around and around, one box to the next, to form a tower of sweet treats tied fast in boxes, the knots tied over and over again for security, the white string a cotton soft against the skin and not overly strong, but strong enough. A very strong person could snap it if they wanted. My mother was strong but she never snapped it, she slid the string off each box and put it in her string drawer, until she had time to sit down, untie the knots one by one, and wind the string into a ball.

If she untied knots on a sunny afternoon it was because she was in a good mood, relaxing while the tomato sauce cooked on the stove. Her long fingers with their polished red nails worked comfortably with the knots, coaxing them to loosen and come enjoy the sunshine, the white cotton string pale against her olive skin, the fibers visibly expanded by her touch. It was a win-win situation — the string stopped its knotting and wound into a ball once again, and my mother enjoyed her afternoon.

When I was a girl I didn't know about her sheep in Italy. How she, at my age, looked after them. It wasn't for many decades that I learned of how she twisted the wool strands from the shorn fleeces into threads for her mother to weave into clothes and every other cloth the family needed.

Now, when I remember my mother untying the knots from the bakery string, I'm reminded of a stained glass window in church, a beautiful image rich in colour and form in its own right, but with an important and marvellous story to be discovered.

My mother, and all my relatives, emigrated from Italy after the First World War. They came by ship, packed into steerage, a long journey with nothing to do. Maybe that's where my mother picked up her love of knots, from the seafaring crew whose knots secured the lifeboats and strapped things down on tumultuous ocean voyages. I doubt she'd had much to do with knots on the farm in Italy. Oh, some simple knots, yes, but the sheep ran free, as did she, and not much in Italy was tied tightly, or needed to be tied together. Time had done most of that, through custom, and ritual, and family.

Some of my relatives, like my mother, absolutely loved North American culture and flourished in it. My mother delighted in the glamour of lipstick, nail polish, exquisite ready-made clothes, which made her look as beautiful as a movie star. From early on, she had her hair done once a week at a beauty parlour where they washed it, set it, and sprayed it into shape for her. She's eighty-six now, and family photos show her hairstyle hasn't changed since she was thirty.

She had found herself when she emigrated from Italy, found her hairstyle, found the red polish she always wore on her long nails that she trimmed and filed religiously. The red nail polish she also stroked onto every pot that she brought to the church for their spaghetti suppers to identify it easily as her own. Found the brilliant red lipstick she wears always, now proudly ordering it from Victoria's Secret. If she sat today untying the knotted string from bakery boxes, she'd look the same as when I was a girl, more grey-haired perhaps, but essentially the same.

We ordered regularly from the bakery, crumb buns every Sunday after Mass, cookies and pastries for Mom's bridge club every Wednesday, coffee cake and cheesecake for visitors, cakes for birthdays, anniversaries, graduations, all the celebrations of our large extended family. The bakery offered scrumptious fare and we enjoyed it often, so there was lots of string with lots of knots to untie.

As we five children in my family and all our cousins grew up, the reasons to bring home treasures from the bakery increased. We celebrated everything together, graduations from kindergarten to high school, birthdays for each of us, wedding anniversaries — celebrating was routine for us. More reasons for cookies, more strudels, more petit fours.

Not that we celebrated only with baked goods, heavens no. We were good Italians — we celebrated with homemade ravioli, with salad, stuffed mushrooms, meatballs and sausages, grapes, pears, nuts, wine, espresso. We celebrated every Sunday after church, every Holy Day, every church event, every family event of any sort. Usually we made our own food. But the string came only from the bakery boxes, special because it was part of the North American culture. In the Italian villages, there were no bakeries; villagers made their own bread, and rarely baked anything sweet. There were no boxes, there was no string. Boxes and string were luxuries of the New World. My mother appreciated everything about North America. The string was a North American bonus and only tied her more closely to the new culture.

Everything in the New World was as they had dreamed, beautiful houses, beautiful children well-dressed, well-schooled, a church full of saints and candles where the women all wore hats and gloves, where all the shoes were shined, all the faces scrubbed clean. In homes, picture windows amazingly graced the living rooms of ordinary people not just the wealthy. There were pianos, too, in many houses on any street, children took lessons after school or on Saturdays, they had recitals, played the classics, set off on lives so obviously better than villages in Italy could offer. There were spelling bees and mathematics. There were science fairs and essay contests with awards announced in the local paper. Life was good and would only get better.

My mother would sit at the kitchen table dressed, as always, quite nicely in that 1950's way, never in slacks, always in a sweater and skirt, stockings and heels, the bakery string in knotted bundles on the Formica tabletop, a soft smile on her face as she worked at loosening the knots, remembering the celebrations where the sweets had been enjoyed. Remembering her daughters dressed in chiffons and velvets, all four wearing matching dresses, little hats, white gloves, patent leather shoes, dream clothing tied at the back with bows. The knots were not knots for her to untangle as much as rosary beads to finger recalling memories of bows. Her memories in the cells of her skin, her life had made her happy.

As children leave home they dream their own dreams and strangers dream dreams for them. But the hand-off from parents to others isn't a clean break, not so tidy as a sentence might imply. It's as tangled, as twisted, as the bakery string knots, a maze of pathways, some leading to opportunities, some to dead ends, some to unimagined futures.

My mother untangled the bakery string in those days of change, too. Her own appearance as tidy as ever — stockings and heels, a sweater and skirt, hair done, lips red, nails filed and polished, earrings glinting real gold — she was Mary Immaculate. No doubt of her own path whatsoever, but sink holes all around her to test that faith. My mother believed in herself absolutely, confident in her good sense and her intuition. But her daughters weren't all like her. We stumbled where she might have been sure footed. Maybe she got her sense and balance from her sheep in Italy. Maybe she was born fearless. Certainly she made the transition from shepherdess to Lady of the New World easily, more easily than either her own mother or her daughters.

Like so many Italian immigrants, her mother was homesick, sad because she was a rootless stranger here, sad because her children were embarrassed by her. My grandmother lived with us in my mother's house after years of being in charge of her own house — and farm — in Italy. Here, in her daughter's house, rugs covered every floor, rugs that couldn't be scrubbed clean like the stone floors in Conca. It was a house cleaned by machines that roared like monsters — the vacuum, washing machine, dishwasher — war-like cleaning machines that made the scrubbing and sweeping of Italian housecleaning seem soothing. This house was fancy, a house that could be hurt in so many ways. There were things to break, spill, ruin. My grandmother did them all, and my mother was infuriated with her.

My grandmother tried to be happy but needed more than bakery treats to be satisfied. She missed her farm in Italy, her groves of hazelnuts and olives, her sheep and horses, her loom for weaving. None were here, none were needed here. She wasn't needed here. Not like in Italy where she was essential, where she was full of life, a life-giver. Transplanted here, she was just another knot to unravel, a problem for her children, unproductive and old before her time.

My mother wanted everyone to delight in the New World. She grew angry at Grandma — furious with her — for being unhappy. They argued in Italian, and Grandma was sent to live with one of my mother's sisters. First to Aunt Angie, to Aunt Josie after that. Grandma became a problem. She prayed more;

she wept; she learned to use the phone and phoned her busy daughters at their work, lonely, with nothing to do and no one to talk to.

Her daughters worked with their husbands in the stores they owned, the grocery, the confectionery, the tailor shop, the children all in school, Grandma alone all day, no one, not even a baby, to talk to. Italy a dream that, if ever forgotten, pitched her off the edge of the Earth into the oblivion of the obsolete. My mother could not see it. It was too dangerous. In my mother's mind, everything was marvelous. Everything had to be marvelous.

And so, my mother continued to untie the knots recalling all the celebrations, the wedding anniversaries, birthdays, graduations from grade eight, graduations from high school, but in with those wondrous celebrations, she also had to think about Grandma, and the growing difficulties she seemed to have. The knots unraveled more easily when my mother was recalling the joyous occasions. When she thought about Grandma, the knots seemed tighter.

Then the children, growing and grown, jumped into motorboats and sped away. Not like my mother's ocean liner full of immigrants with plans and dreams, nothing as long-term as that. These were whimsical jaunts, quickies with seemingly no consequences, or none planned for. As my mother untied knots at the kitchen table a line crept across her brow, gradually she could see outcomes unanticipated and severe. Mates, grandchildren, broken marriages, second marriages, unexpectedly expanding the family and calling for impromptu boxes of cookies and treats.

Some say one can always find reason for celebration if a fearless search is made. Knots can be untied, string re-rolled and good again, knotted bundles softened and smoothed like new. The string drawer eventually grew empty, all the celebrations over and done with. All the Old Ones gone, all the young ones grown and moved away. The New World not so new anymore. Once immigration starts, it's easier and easier to move away again, easier and easier to untie from the dock and drift, easier for an object in motion to stay in motion. Ties to Italy loosen more every day. Memories become a thing of the past. My mother sits at Sunrise Lodge with no bundles of knotted string to untie, wondering what became of her string drawer. Most of the other relatives untied from this Earth and headed for Heaven long ago. Every child and grandchild has moved a world away.

When we visit, we bring her sweets thinking she'll like that. But I wonder if she does.

CARS OF MY HEART

TWO CARS SIT IN MY DRIVEWAY. "ONE FOR each hand" my neighbour jokes, since I live alone. They're both white Toyotas, the smaller one I bought new sixteen years ago at the urging of my youngest son when he was fifteen and proud to be helpful and caring. I loved that car long after he'd grown and moved away because it was such a good car, good like the son who chose it for me. I treated it well, looked after it, plugged it in even if the temperature was only ten below, kept the gas tank full, never let it go too long without an oil change. I brought that car back to the Toyota dealership itself for servicing, even though it cost more. I believe that was proper, to take it back to the maker, to let those who knew it best look after it.

Then I collapsed, a stroke of the clock, a stroke in my brain and I had to hire people to drive me if I had to go anywhere far, or go somewhere where there was too much traffic for my new confusion to handle, and that's when damage was done to my dear car, by newcomers who weren't in it for the long haul, who would take charge of my car and snap things off and let things get too hot, their hands like bombs. People trying to help who hurt without knowing it. Not that they didn't care, they just didn't care enough. It's what happens when you entrust your own to others. Not caring enough always has consequences, not looking after things steadfastly hastens decline. Oh sure, everything declines and dies sooner or later, but sooner rather than later if uncared for.

My mother is in a senior's home and that's the way it is with her, too — the staff kindly enough, but not family, not relevant, not related to the past. It's like the difference between a home cooked Italian meal and an Italian restaurant meal. You pay for the restaurant meal, you pay for the restaurant's ambiance, and as good as it might be, it's just not like home. Mama's smiles, Aunt Josie's warmth, their hands forming the meatballs or handling the pizza dough, memories of Italy come fill their hearts while they stand at the stove, stirring, tasting, thinking of us — all these ingredients combine with their ancestral belief in the goodness of food prepared for family, to make our meals blessed and full of grace as well as delicious.

Not that everything has to be Italian, it's just that our family is, so we appreciate Italian touchstones to help us remember who we are. That's what happens to immigrants, we feel desolate, lonely for our ancestors separated from us by time, space, pop culture, plastics, and rock and roll; separated from the profound and sacred meanings of familiar things like bread and wine. Immigrants lose the poetry of life, the insights gained by lifetimes of attentiveness to the relationships between things. Survival in a stranger's culture makes us too literal: "How do you say . . . ?" "Where is . . . ?" "What's funny . . . ?" Life without poetry can be terribly trying.

How about this: life is like a ball of wool, round and rolling — everybody understands wool, right? Things like buttons and brooches are pretty add-ons, but not part of the weave that makes a thing a thing. My mother in a senior's home is like a sweater in a dryer, warm and quite fine in there, just tumbled about in the course of time.

When we're with her, my brother, my sisters, all part of the same wool, the wool from her sheep in Italy, same colour, same memory, same language, we all know where Conca is, her hometown, and if needed, could transplant her there if she asked. I might pick her up in my little car that's sitting next to the newer one in my driveway, or at least I could have picked her up before the strokes, and we would all together travel to the airport and fly across the ocean with her, we sisters bringing food in our purses, my brother contributing a box of Italian pastries from his favourite bakery, smiles on our faces, happy to be together, happy to fly Mom back home.

That will happen someday, maybe not in this lifetime, but someday. All of us, back on Italian soil. All of us together in the village church, heads bowed, glad to be home, saying to ourselves and each other, *what were we thinking leaving this place, where were we going an age ago, how could we not see what would happen?* Time and generations are merely picky details; in essence, the past, present, and future, are one in the blood, never ending, unlimited. Her home, our home, because we are hers. Her leaving, our leaving, because we are hers. The staff in the senior's home just smile at my mother and move along nicely to the next old lady they're to look after, their blood olive-free and disconnected from us and our past, from us and our future.

The newer car in my driveway is new to me but not brand new, and I don't know that car. I'm afraid it will die in my hands. The previous owners loved it, but one had cancer and passed on, and the other moved to New Zealand where they drive on the other side of the road. These previous owners had a garage, kept their car, now my car, in their garage. I bought a car accustomed to the comfort of a garage, but I have no garage. What was I thinking? They had it serviced at the Toyota dealership, just like me — one similarity at last. Japanese cars for Italians and Presbyterians alike.

In fact, that's where we met, at the Toyota dealership. The woman was having her car, now my car, serviced before selling it; I was there because my car was having troubles born of a well-meaning driver-for-hire. The woman who owned her car, now my car, had the oil changed and the car inspected and the Toyota Man leaned towards her in confidence whispering what a good car it was and how she would have no trouble selling it, especially for the price she was asking. I was eavesdropping, very rude *mea culpa* and Heaven was telling me to pay attention.

At least I thought it was Heaven, my people in Heaven. Lots of my relatives there — Aunt Josie, Uncle Nick, (three Uncle Nicks actually), and both sets of Grandmas and Grandpas, everyone gathered and telling me *take the car, take the car,* just like on a game show. Then I learned much later, the lady who owned her car/my car was a Reverend, a Presbyterian Reverend, active, working in the Church, so maybe it was *her* folks in Heaven cheering me on to buy her car, trying to help her out so she could take the Kiwi Express to New Zealand worry free.

Could I have mistaken her heavenly allies for mine? I doubt it. My relatives are so distinctive in Heaven and elsewhere, warm blooded, gold and olive and red in colour, excited, smiling with their eyebrows raised and a glass of wine lifted. In our family, we smile generously, our smiles littering our lives like cherry blossoms. I don't know what other Presbyterians are like in Heaven or on Earth, but the Presbyterian minister at the Toyota dealership didn't look like any relative of mine.

When my aunts dressed up, they would wear the deluxe dresses of North American culture in their enthusiastic attempts to fit in. Any wedding footage shows them wearing hats and high heeled shoes, tiny belts around their waists, outfitted to be as glamorous as movie stars. Or at church trying to be respectable in modest dresses with jackets, hats with veils, their dark hands covered by smooth white gloves. But do they fit in? Nope. They are too round, too brown, too exuberant. The women, my women, flow across the borders of their fancy dresses and their churchly-modest suits, the men choke in noose-like ties and stuff the square suits on their rounded forms to the bursting point.

I can't give up on them because they don't look right to others; they look perfect to me. Beautiful. Everyone else pales in comparison. In my memory, my people, in church or out of church, radiate earthy exuberance. Daily life made them so happy — I always remember them smiling — unless they were crying at a funeral, smiling came easily to them.

This car, now my car, made the Presbyterian minister lady happy, she was fond of her car, now my car. But for me, it was not love at first sight. I understand love at first sight, it's in my blood. But there's no love involved in this car transaction, it's just a convenient good deal. My young son doesn't sit in the backseat watching over me. I'm not smitten, I don't see my aunts and uncles waving from the porch, yearning for rides in the backseat.

I worry because when I look at the Presbyterian minister's car, it leaves me cold. And on top of that, I can't give it the luxury of a warm garage. If I loved it, love would be all I could give, love with no garage. The Presbyterian minister wasn't Italian, she was not a love-at-first-sight person, she was careful, measured, quiet, calm. This car is used to her. But I'm not used to her or her car. I try and imagine what the world is like for her. Not an immigrant; she belonged. It must be wonderful to belong. Can I, with my transplanted Italian peasant persona, immigrate into her world and fit in with her car? If I have no idea how she lives her life, is it really possible for me to drive her car? Is her life as it seems to be — colder, harder, less sweet — or is it something else that my immigrant soul does not understand yet? I think we immigrants easily lose our wisdom of how the world works. Being transplanted is a psychic root canal, and no fun.

That car is out there right now in my driveway, twenty degrees below zero, not in a garage like the previous owner would have had it, not tucked, not pampered, but out there in the elements and suffering at my hand — or is it anxious to come to me, finally getting to experience a new life, it's engine hungry as a sled dog to kick up heat when I finally start it again? Hungry as my grandfathers were at the thought of crossing the ocean to life in the New World, innocent of the consequences to their desires?

Fire runs hot in our blood, we are the people of Vesuvius, exuberant ones who dare to sop up every juicy drop of life, and God Himself knows and loves it. That's why he put the Pope in Rome — to be near us. He likes us. Look at the world — God doesn't stay in the lines when He colours and neither do we. In fact the lines aren't straight in God's world. Not one. There are curves and wobbles and detours everywhere. The one thing God DIDN'T create was the straight line. Everything else, yes, but not that.

So I have two cars in my driveway, both Toyotas, one I've had for sixteen years, the other for sixteen days. And I must choose which to keep, which to sell.

At least that was the case until the phone rang. A young man, soft-voiced, needs a car because of a new baby and he heard about mine through Jeff. Oh yes, Jeff. Not that I ever spoke to Jeff about my car, but in this small town, no doubt somebody spoke to somebody who spoke to Jeff. And as I listen to this soft-voiced young man, I like him instantly, and he needs to go pick up stuff for his cat that he had to have fixed because of the new baby, so I offer to loan him my car, sight unseen. He's coming to pick it up shortly. Things sure can change in the ring of a phone. I know he'll want the car, and I'll say yes of course. Certainly my sixteen-year-old happy car will want to go with the soft-voiced young man and his wife, baby, and cat. Who wouldn't want to go along with that group? I myself am inclined to adopt them as my own.

Which leaves me with the Presbyterian minister's car. I wonder about this . . . this . . . this . . . marriage.

It reminds me of the marriages of my sisters and my brother (all of us have had several). None of us has ever married an Italian, not one homemade match, and I wonder what went through my parents' minds during those years of the courtships of their children. Didn't marry Italians, didn't marry Catholics, Mom and Dad saw each of us drive away in cars owned by atheists, Protestants, drunks, social workers. No sibling spouse was ever blood of our blood, spirit of our spirits, none with our customs, our food, our happiness, none will have anything to do with us in Heaven once we all get there. After what they've been through, my parents would not be surprised to see a Presbyterian car parked in my driveway. They heard my beautiful name/their name changed to a foreign one, they heard their grandsons called by that name as well. All my sisters, too, discarding my parents' beautiful generous Italian name full of a's and o's to take German names, Irish names, Slovak names. A Presbyterian car in my driveway would be less than a surprise.

It's Saint Patrick's Day. When I was in grade five at Saint Elizabeth school we had a talent show. I played the piano. They introduced me as Donna O'Caruso. Changed my name to suit their occasion. During rehearsal, the Irish-ized names weren't used, they came as a surprise for the performance. Like the Presbyterian lady's hand-off at the Toyota dealership. Life's sometimes like that, suddenly I'm changed, my name is not my name, my car is not my car, events conspire to repaint me as something other than I am. Never for a moment would I have predicted being this closely associated with a Presbyterian. Intimately close, sitting where she sat, holding the wheel where her hands held it, looking into her rearview mirror. I haven't cleaned it, haven't wiped her away. Her fingerprints still press into surfaces, her exhaled breath still fills the air, her radio stations still play even though she's on the other side of the world where day is night and up is down. I'm where she was, stepping into her Presbyterian shoes.

We're expected to know things, but I never know them. Even the small things make me sweat. My mother knows everything; no one is as sure as she is — except my father. I must have been adopted because my veins are completely devoid of the certainty they brought to every moment of their lives. They never doubted a single thing. Certainty was one of the things my parents loved about each other. They could decide the grandiose and the miniscule with total ease: where to go for lunch, what to order, what time to leave, what to wear, how to build a business and make it grow and flourish. They could have ruled a country; they could have ruled the world, so sure and wise they were. But not me. I guess they took all the certainty and I took the discarded doubt they didn't need. They urged me always to stop thinking so much. I'm open to far too many possibilities; they know exactly what they want. Even if they don't get what they want they know what it was they wanted. Certainty gives you what you want because the line is clear: you want this, it belongs to you.

Like my mother's luck in gambling. She always wins. Today she's having rather serious surgery for heart problems; she'll do fine. She'll say a prayer, of course, but she knows that she'll do fine. The last time she had heart surgery she did fine. Because her prayers were answered, yes, but also because the surgery is on Thursday, her poker day. She always wins at poker, she always wins at surgery on Thursdays. She'd win even if it weren't her poker day, but she's all the more certain of winning on her poker Thursday.

But some of us, like me, don't know what to ask for when we pray, and don't have much luck at poker either. So maybe God tired of me praying generous prayers for the good health and good luck of others: make so-and-so happy, bring so-and-so good health, I hope so-and-so finds someone to love. I bet God wanted to hear me just once say: give me a winning hand, make the damage from the strokes go away, give me a great car at a price I can afford. It's like Sears points. You get them when you buy things from Sears, but if you don't use them in time you lose them. So maybe God or the Cosmos or my Guardian Angel just got staggeringly tired of my points slipping away and this Presbyterian minister lady was corralled to hand off her excellent car to me so that I'd finally release my old one to the young couple who seem an awful lot like the Holy Family on a donkey in a stable, in need of reliable transportation.

The doorbell just rang. It's the soft-voiced young man here to pick up the keys to my dear old car of sixteen years. He'll pay me and drive off into the sunset with his wife and new baby and together the family will bring home their cat from the vet's.

I'll resign myself to making friends with this foreign car, this Presbyterian Toyota, not a single breadcrumb of Italian culture to guide or comfort me. My stomach knots from the strangeness of this experience. When my mother moved into the seniors home after my father died, resigning herself to the whims of those paid to care for her instead of us, her family, I wonder how she felt. I wonder if, for her, the first uncertainty of her life came then. And maybe the truth for me is this, that the turmoil

I encounter in embracing this Presbyterian car drives me, in mysterious ways, to understand my mother better. The eddies and undercurrents of life make experiences hauntingly complex and sometimes buying a car not really about buying a car at all. It seems to be part of the "no straight lines" thing.

I need to learn about the ways of the Presbyterian, of the non-Italian who drives and cares for cars, and I need to learn the ways of gods who force goodness on us whether we believe in it or not. And I need to see that my mother may have known uncertainty after all, and been more like me than I have ever imagined.

Mirror Image

My mother's wardrobe posed in readiness — luscious silks, fine woolens, imports from Italy and Ireland, a long steady row crammed into both sides of her enormous double-doored closet, pressed one behind the other, bodices against backs, shoulder to gorgeous shoulder, breathtakingly tight, like a line of smiling Beauty Queens all packed together for a group photo, beautiful, elegant, ready to dazzle unreservedly once given more space.

Then there was the white leather jewelry box on her vanity, so full of pearls and golden things it had to remain open day and night. Daily she would sit in front of the large mirror to put on her earrings. She'd fasten one, then the other, approving and pleased with how she looked, she'd smile at her reflection. For me, this ritual adornment was like Van Gogh's myriad self portraits, repetitive, simple, beautiful, and holy.

In the evening she would return her earrings to the jewelry box, slip on her red silk robe, and manicure her long fingernails, paint them red and her toenails, too, as she sipped Napoleon brandy and watched Claudette Colbert in *Since You Went Away* or Katharine Hepburn and Spencer Tracey in *Pat and Mike*. She had collected many things: corsages, photos, programs from celebratory dinners and receptions — all cherished mementos which made her smile each time she saw them, memories which filled her heart just as these clothes filled this closet, full to overflowing.

The bottom of her closet held shoes in their original boxes, with other shoes hung in shoe trees along the sides of her closet. Her closet was enormous — in third world countries whole families would live in a place as big as my mother's closet. Shoes packed along the floor, hat boxes along the four feet height and eight foot length of the top shelf. Twelve deep and generous drawers held her clothes as well, my poor father assigned just one of those, and that half-empty because as many clothes as my mother accumulated my father didn't, a few shirts, socks, and underwear, all he ever required.

As we grew up and moved out on our own, my mother's wardrobe took over abandoned closets and drawers in every bedroom, ever-growing to fill them all, drawers full of silk scarves, drawers full of leather gloves, of bras, of girdles, slips, blouses, pajamas, belts, everything she ever wore.

Some of my mother's clothes would fit me, others would fit each of my three sisters, even though we were different widths and heights, because in the course of her lifetime my mother's body shrunk and expanded as her life required, as she desired. She saved every piece of clothing regardless of the size, shopping relentlessly all her life, loving how she looked no matter what, her posture tall despite her short frame, tall with the strength of her pride and her absolute love of living her life. She was really like a child in her enjoyment, an elegant child perhaps, but she was glad to be alive, and she dressed the part.

However, a time came when she could no longer live on her own, and she needed a smaller place, a senior's place, one room, simple, safe. The new place would never be big enough for her wardrobe even if nothing else was in it but her clothes, and so, her wardrobe's time of increase ended and the editing began. Each item had a story, some stories stayed, most went.

She had treasures secreted away, classics gathered lovingly over a lifetime. She never easily parted with anything, no matter how old or out of date, so sending her clothing off for world-wide distribution tore at her. Each of us, my mother's four daughters, received something of hers. We all loved her clothes.

There were glorious gowns, both bare and demure at once, like the black taffeta with its long, full skirt which fanned to the floor, as gracious and generous as my mother's round hips. Its strapless bodice, beaded and beautiful, had cupped my mother's breasts and offered them up, sacred flesh that conjured images of Holy Heaven. She had been a goddess in this black dress. The golden silk dress she wore to weddings, the suit she wore when receiving the award from our church, her wedding dress — each of these dresses held memories, and none of us fought over who got what from my mother. My sisters and I were used to rituals and generosity, we had learned a lot of things from my mother, and the sharing of clothing was one of them. "May I have this?" was always answered with "Yes, of course."

ຜ ຜ ຜ

WHEN I WAS THREE OR FOUR, I loved to help my mother do up her garters and stockings. She found the front ones easy to fasten herself, the rubber knob on the garter slipped smoothly under the top of the stocking, the metal fastener slid into place perfectly. The side garters as well, fastening perfectly along the rounded side of her thighs. The back ones were trickier; sometimes they pulled to one side if she wasn't careful because she had to turn and reach backwards to do them up. She stood straight, round and lovely, and let me do those. I would kneel, intimately close, the technology of the garters amazing and wonderful to my little girl fingers. I delicately slid the last of the garters into place so my mother's stockings were fastened secure and straight.

The soft fabrics and her soft skin were one part of a two-part experience. As lovely as her skin and stockings were and all the rest of her clothes, too, I was fascinated by the rubber girdle which restrained her lovely curves. Her entire life she wore a girdle, even when it caused blood clots in her legs, the idea of looking sloppy was something she couldn't bear. She went girdle-less only when she wore pajamas, but at any event where others would be present, she dressed completely, girdle and all.

Dressed, undressed, her body warm and full, a source of pride and pleasure, there was never an ounce of apology in her, no matter what her age or weight, no matter how much silver in the sea of her hair's black waves.

The nuns at my school had hidden their bodies under shapeless layers of cloth, their heads, all their hair, and half their faces wrapped, too. I wondered, as so many of my classmates did, if they had ears, or breasts, or if they ever went to the bathroom. I couldn't imagine them having their periods. But my mother had everything, all her parts in working order. In the worst heat of summer, she would strip, working around the house in her Playtex Longline Bra, her girdle, and her half slip. When the heat soared, she'd even come to the supper table dressed in a bathing suit. My father would object but that was too bad. If she was hot she would cool down whatever way she could. If she wanted to take off clothing, she would. She had nothing to be ashamed of. Ever.

I remember trying on my mother's clothing — satins, organza, and fabrics I can't even name, fabrics foreign to my adult wardrobe. I never felt right in my mother's clothes, too fancy, too beautiful, too formal for my girdle-less shape. Her clothes were quintessentially not me, but evocative of her presence so that she appeared in my mind in any of her clothing that I tried on, sometimes she was youthful, sometimes older, smelling gorgeous in her perfume, absolutely glowing in the joy of her dressed-up self.

I used to watch her apply her makeup and perfume, the blend of scents so enticing it made you want to hold her close and inhale as if she were a flower. When my mother slipped into her dress, careful not to muss up her hair, careful not to smear her makeup, she would swim through the circle of the skirt with a long and knowing stroke, passing it over her head and down her body like a magician proving a woman who floated in mid-air was there by magic. Then she would pull the dress around her body, lifting her breasts, hugging the waist of the dress to her own, and she would have someone do up the zipper for her.

My father usually had the honours when he himself was dressed up to take her out. And when he did up her zipper there was always a moment, the two of them standing before the mirror, her hands holding her dress to her small waist, and my father behind her attending to the technology of the zipper; a moment when he would look up at the mirror, and my mother's beauty would seduce him anew. Their eyes would lock, shining with love, and he would gather her in his arms and kiss the back of her neck.

ℰ ℰ ℰ

My mother had mountains of shoes, handbags, and scarves from her entire life of shopping. Although none were ever discarded, she still shopped for more. Shopping revitalized her, she loved it. Her body delighted in being treated to new things whatever they were. Even the silk long johns she wore later in life under her winter trousers were a joy to buy. Her sensuous clothing made her feel that life was delicious and gentle, elegant and painless. She forgot all sadnesses and hardships if she wrapped her body in beauty. That centred her, connected her to the goodness of God. When my sisters and I wear my mother's clothes or shoes, when we carry her handbags, we feel her with us, and see her in each other. We don't look very much like her, but her spirit is evident.

I have folded each satin, each velvet, folded each slip and each silk blouse, every dress for day or evening, every sweater, every scarf to keep as a treasure. What I have fills a single suitcase. My sisters took more than I, but still, only suitcases full of dresses, jewelry, scarves, hats, gloves. A large truck was required to take away the rest. Everything folded and boxed, everything for the Salvation Army. The shipment was astonishing in its size. Even the corporal who did the pick up was impressed.

"Thank you for thinking of us," he said.

The red and black van drove off. My mother's clothes would be her surrogate ashes, they would scatter across the earth, bringing bits of her to here, to there, to those not fortunate enough to have known her in life. No memorial service, no commemorative Mass, nothing could be more appropriate a ritual.

❦ ❦ ❦

Her closet is empty now, the back wall exposed, the floor shoeless and uncluttered, the overhead shelf devoid of hat boxes. Even the hangers have gone, to the Salvation Army. Anyone would think that surely there was nothing left. But lives don't clear as easily as that.

I keep her things, the ones she gave me, the ones I asked for because my memories of her wearing them are strongest. They are together in storage, a plain brown wrapper of a shrine. But she could never be contained or confined, that was obvious throughout her life, and certainly not now, when her daughters are grown and thinking of her more every day.

I see her sometimes when I look in the mirror, especially when I put on earrings and recall each time she did that same ritual at her vanity. Out of the corner of my eye, always on the periphery of my vision, is my mother, dressed and smiling, a familiar face.

In Burying An Italian Mother

SOME PEOPLE CAN BE CREMATED WITHOUT A second thought. If they're dead, light the fire and be done with it. No fuss, no funeral, no fiddling around with plots, grave maintenance, or letters chiseled in granite. But cremation for my mother? That would be a sin against her nature. When she dies, we're to have a nice dinner party, not a barbecue. An Italian woman, mother of five, who started her life in Italy as a shepherdess, who grew up in the strong arms and watchful eyes of the mountaintop villagers south of Naples, she could never be cremated.

Until not very long ago, the Italian Popes condemned cremation as a funeral pyre that sent you straight to the fires of Hell. They required burial in the earth, a proper burial in the cemetery adjacent to the village church. My mother would understand. Throughout her whole life her body has savoured fresh-pressed olive oil and exquisite vine-ripened tomatoes. She has grown her own garden and delighted in fresh salads, she has prepared roasted red peppers, fennel, escarole for her family and friends, has *saluted* every meal and every celebration with red wine. An Italian woman like my mother must feast her death as she did her life. No quick and casual barbecue, no funeral pyre.

Her instructions are clear: we must arrange for a wooden casket draped with fresh flowers. We must select a beautiful dress, pouf her hair as if she were going someplace nice. We must bring her to my father's side, to where she lay all her life since she was sixteen, to where the consecrated ground marked with her name welcomes her to her last home.

Her grandsons, amongst her pall bearers, will walk her to that spot where Heaven begins for her. They will honour the memory of their grandmother and their grandfather, and the memory of all their ancestors who live on within the bones and blood of our family here on Earth. We will have no ashes to sprinkle over landscapes. Their grandmother, my mother, will be buried in the soil, immersed in it. She will disassemble into it, and come alive again another way, her earthen eyes and mouth, her heart of mud warmed once again by sunshine and blooming into flowers, berries, blades of grass.

Her name will be engraved on her gravestone, her memory engraved forever in space and time. Shovelfuls of sorrow and forgiveness chant the song of her burial. More than half of all the people she shared in life will welcome her on the other side. She will be glad to see them, though sad to leave us here. My father, smiling, will embrace his one true love. Even her sheep greet her and call to her there.

Those of us, those of her line, believe in this: that Heaven is run by an Italian God, a God who loves a table full of relatives, whose big kitchen always has drawers full of spoons and aprons, cupboards full of plates, counters full of aromatic onions, scallions, tomatoes, and peppers, always the smell of something wonderful cooking. There's a garden in the backyard, a wine cellar in the basement. It gets noisy in Heaven with cousins, aunts, and uncles, but it is a holy place because the people there remember the oceans of foolishness and promise that make up this sweet life on earth and cherish every moment they spent here.

Heaven has room for us all. My mother will be happy there. She will join in with the angels singing, she will smile at God and ask Him if He'd like a few more ziti. In Heaven, she will be what she was on Earth — at home. So no crematory fire for her as if she desperately needed purging of her life, as if the Earth had polluted her spirit, as if the body once dead had no life in it, as if all flesh and blood required purification by fire. Set her to rest in the rich brown Earth. Peasant stock trusts the Earth, has no quarrel with the Earth. And no one loves Heaven more than those of us who love the Earth.

ANGELS AND SAINTS

Angels and Saints

Aunt Josie made ravioli on her and Uncle Nick's double bed for every family gathering at her home. She'd cover their bed with a clean linen tablecloth, then put her three-foot-wide wooden board and her six-foot-long rolling pin on it, along with a bowl full of the dough, and another bowl full of the ricotta cheese and parsley filling that she'd made up in the kitchen. She had another smaller bowl of loose flour to scatter on the board so she could keep the dough from sticking, and she let me watch her make the ravioli.

Aunt Josie made cheese ravioli, never meat ravioli. Her ravioli patties measured about three or four inches across, entirely unlike the tiny little one inch, doughy squares that you get in a tin can. Aunt Josie's ravioli dough got lighter and lighter as she got older and older, so that in her later life you could eat an entire bowlful of ravioli, about six or seven enormous patties, and not feel full. It was a miracle our family witnessed and for which we thanked Aunt Josie, God, and all the Angels in Heaven who surely assisted her in her kitchen. Aunt Josie loved cooking so much she envisioned spending eternity cooking for those who lived in God's House, and when she passed on we thought we heard a cheer go up amongst the cherubim and all the other angels in welcome for her.

The saints, too, must have smiled to learn Josie had arrived, with her favourite saint, Saint Anthony, guiding her through the Pearly Gates. All her life, she had liked him, even more than she liked Cary Grant who was a Hollywood dreamboat. Saint Anthony was in charge of finding things for people, and he'd answered Aunt Josie's prayers countless times helping to find lost articles for her and her family. Now she was home in Heaven, and he had helped her find her way — straight to her heavenly kitchen.

She left her mark on the world in many ways besides her cooking and her prayers to Saint Anthony. In her dry cleaning business, Aunt Josie was a stain-removing superhero, vanquishing sordid smudges from every sort and every type of fabric. One time I watched as she took the indelible ballpoint ink marks out of a lace tablecloth, a stain that had been in the lace for several years. She dipped the ink in milk and it disappeared like magic. We applauded when we saw it. If spilled coffee was black, it washed out easily, if it had milk in it, that was more difficult to remove, but Aunt Josie could do it. She could do anything. At suppertime, if red wine was knocked onto a white linen tablecloth, she salted the wine-soaked area and the stain vanished in the wash the next day.

Aunt Josie made the world a cleaner, neater, tastier place. When we lost her, we wept and smiled all at once because we understood that she had couriered bits of Heaven to us, shown us the coming attractions. She was a trailer for the afterlife to make us want to go see it. Aunt Josie went up ahead of us to get things ready. She's likely making ravioli as we speak.

Aunte Josie and Uncle Nick

He rolled his eyes and clowned around, grabbed her and hugged her tight. That was Nick. She blushed and shooshed him away, never one to admit she liked his attention. Nick married Josie because they rode the subway together to work in the same dressmaking factory in the 1930s. If you spent that much time with someone riding back and forth to work, everyone expected you would get married. And they did get married; Josie the seamstress married Nick the tailor, and they lived ever after as husband and wife.

Josie had been eighteen when she immigrated to the New World with her family, leaving not only Italy behind but a young man she liked so much she had kissed him — often. Kissed him so much she nearly had to marry him. And would have married him had he asked her, but her parents were already packing and arguing about moving to the New World when he popped the question, and her mother wasn't about to leave Josie an ocean away with a new husband. They boarded the ship and Aunt Josie never heard from her young man again.

This heartbreak left Aunt Josie restless, furtive, busy at all times so as not to think too much about her sweetheart in Italy. Perhaps she expected him to follow, to show up on her doorstep with a new proposal of marriage. If he loved her as she loved him would he not follow? Surely he knew how she felt about him. She would already be married and pregnant had she not crossed the ocean with her family to ride the subway every day with Nick. The ocean crossing was hardest on Josie, my mother says she was seasick the entire time of the crossing, turning green, crying, and vomiting the whole way over.

Josie's older brother, Alberto, befriended Nick, introduced Nick to Josie, and all three rode the subway to the factory to work six days a week. When your brother's best friend is as endearing and as much fun as Nick, it's difficult to ignore him. Nick greeted Josie every morning, his bright brown eyes sparkling as he said, "Hello Darling". He may not have been her first choice, but he was a nice man.

They fit together in some ways, Josie was a cook and Nick was a hungry man. He appreciated her excellent meals every day of his life. When, in later years, Josie would go into the hospital for weeks at a time, Nick would close the tailor shop at the end of the day and then wander the streets for a place to eat supper. His sighs deep, his expressive brown eyes showed the emptiness of the world without Josie to cook for him, Nick would walk aimlessly to one restaurant one night, another restaurant the next night, to the supper tables of relatives as often as he could garner an invitation. What he found was that no one could equal his Josephina. He missed her terribly.

Uncle Nick, an excellent tailor, could cut fabric with uncanny precision. His workmanship in alterations and pattern making excelled. Here again Nick and Josie meshed in their compatibility: Uncle Nick examined a garment by looking at its seams to evaluate the workmanship. Aunt Josie simply made the inside as beautiful as the outside. They opened Nick's Tailor Shop and Dry Cleaners, a tiny shop where they worked together every day for forty years, Nick made and altered men's suits, Josie hemmed ladies dresses and pressed all the clothes perfectly.

At the tailor shop, Aunt Josie sat on a stool sewing hems, the garment held carefully in her thin strong hands. She sewed small precise stitches to keep the hem in place, her work beautiful to examine, one stitch as tiny and even as the next. She sewed by hand threading the needle and knotting the thread, fast in her work, serious, but always smiling. Nick was at her side working the treadle sewing machine or standing at the cutting table, tailors' shears in hand.

Josie used the huge antique pressing machine at the far end of the narrow shop, a behemoth of a boiler as tall as a truck that clanked and boomed as it exhaled steam like a dragon. Their shop was on our route to school and we always cut through to wish them good morning and to exit via the back door where the dragon's breath would billow around our legs and send us faster on our way.

Nick and Josie had only one child, a son, Louie. Josie didn't have any more children and she wanted a girl, so poor Louie had long baloney curls until he was seven years old. Then he started school and the nuns made Aunt Josie cut Louie's hair. But every Halloween for many years Louie dressed as a girl — one time as Carmen Miranda, with rosied cheeks and a fruit basket hat. He grew up gloriously free, a guy with the best sense of humor ever, sexually straight but completely delightful, and, ironically, he managed a men's clothing store.

One Sunday after Mass when I was about thirteen years old, we all sat around the table having breakfast. Nick, Josie, and Louie were there, as well as all the other usual family members that lived close by. Plans for the afternoon included my family going to our new cottage for the day, my father happy to get out on the water to fish. Nick announced he and Josie would have a picnic on their new land. This surprised us all. Land? Uncle Nick and Aunt Josie didn't have any land; they were rather poor.

Nick announced that he and Josie had purchased cemetery plots, and would have a picnic to enjoy the land from this side before it was time to be on the other side. We all laughed, Aunt Josie, too, even though she lightly slapped Uncle Nick's arm to tell him to stop joking with everyone. She liked him, we all liked him, you couldn't help but like him. He rolled his eyes and wiggled his eyebrows as he smiled and fluttered his long eyelashes. What's not to like?

Aunt Josie was always the first to wish someone well, always the first to volunteer her services as cook or seamstress, always the first to say something nice in an awkward situation. Nick was funny. His son, Louie, inherited his father's sense of humour and his mother's sense of making the best of any situation. As a family, they coursed with energy — smart, happy, funny, well-intentioned. Whatever struggles they might have had were minimized by the goodness of their natures.

A time came when Aunt Josie went into a senior's home where she lived for several years before she died. Nick couldn't care for her, so off she went. They lived apart. That was sad. With stomach trouble that made it difficult for her to eat, Josie went down to about sixty-five pounds. Nick, too, lost weight without Josie to cook for him. He would visit her in the old folks home, but he wouldn't move there, they didn't have rooms for couples. And how could he eat institutional food? Canned soups, canned vegetables, French fries.

Nick lived a decade longer than Josie, on his own in a senior's apartment building where he greeted each woman he saw with a warm-hearted, "Hello, Darling," and hoped to be invited for a good home-cooked meal. When he died, he was buried beside Josie in their cemetery plots. Side by side for all time they will be Josie and Nick, Nick and Josie — you couldn't live together for as long as they did without being buried together.

For Nick, finding the woman who could feed him so well for so long no doubt made him happy. For Aunt Josie, finding a man as funny as Nick was a plus, many women fared far worse than she did. When two people marry for life, they weave, they hem, they tailor their lives and the lives around them. Nick rolled his eyes, Josie said kind things, their son, Louie, wore baloney curls and learned to laugh at life.

Italians On the Landscape

Mr. Guiliano cut the grass with a push mower regularly even in the hottest weather so the lawn looked as beautiful as anyone's, even the church's. He trimmed every edge, every remote corner. We'd see him out in the backyard from the upstairs window over the store, see his huge hands working delicately with the hand clippers along the lengthy wall that separated the raised lawn from the driveway, along the hedges, along the rose beds, trees, and bushes, his strong, over-sized hands snipping every blade to the right height. Nothing used in the garden was motorized in those days; the sounds we heard were almost a silence of snip snip, snip snip, and sighs from Mr. Guiliano bending over, measuring, and trimming.

My father would bring him a glass of beer half way through the job so Mr. Guiliano could have a rest and refresh himself. They'd chat for a while about how the yard looked, what the weather had been like, how the family was doing. As they talked, Mr. Guiliano would reach into his back pocket for a white cloth handkerchief, the kind that all the men of the time carried with them — this was in the days before tissues, when cloth was used for everything — and he would mop the sweat from his brow as he relaxed.

We kids loved to watch Mr. Guiliano work, an older man with a beautiful broad face, the oversized ears and nose that marked his age like the girth of an old tree, a man who sweated and smiled a lot, who our father told us not to bother, but who seemed to enjoy having us around as he looked after our yard. When we got a little older, we mowed the lawn with the push mower ourselves, wondering silently what happened to Mr. Guiliano, but never asking.

Our backyard always looked beautiful, beckoning us to roll on the grass, to gather in the sunshine. We had Sunday picnics every single summer weekend when we children were growing up and our parents were working in their stores. My father and uncles would barbecue, my mother would make a pitcher of peaches in red wine, Aunt Josie would bring a salad and some pasta with meatballs and sausage, Aunt Angie would bring fruit and nuts for desert and sometimes zeppoli, my father would tap a keg of beer, and the wasps would drift over from their nests to join us.

Grandma sat in a wooden lawn chair in the shade, quietly fingering her rosary beads as always. She had lots to pray about and even a family picnic wouldn't stop her. She prayed, I think, for a miracle, to return to her home in Italy which she'd never wanted to leave in the first place, and which she missed more and more every day, especially when seeing her daughters wearing shorts, tightly fitted tops, and red lipstick, their hair bobbed and sprayed at the beauty parlour. Her own hair remained full length, ever-uncut, braided into a bun each morning; her own dresses modest in their cut and length, never once in her life had she worn pants like a man, even though she had run a farm and raised her children in Italy while my grandfather left her for his mistress, the New World.

Uncle Nick Capozzoli loved wearing shorts and a summer shirt, his knobby knees bobbing beneath his nicely rounded belly. Uncle Nick arrived with a smile and the bacchi balls, ready to play. All the adults were good bacchi players, but the men were the best, and Uncle Nick the best of the men. Because there were so many kids, each team had to have several of us. We were awful at playing but that was not a problem, it just meant our teammates had to be that much better to make up for the points we missed.

One after the other, the bacchi balls rolled along the well-trimmed lawn trying to get close to the little ball, the *ballina*. First to one end of the lawn, then to the other, we would pitch the *ballina*, then try in turn to throw each of the bigger balls close to it. Cheers and moans raised at each throw, points counted at each end, the grand prize my mother's pitcher of peaches in wine. The winners always swore they would not share their delicious prize, rolling their eyes and smacking their lips to accentuate how delicious it was, but they always relented after teasing the losers and relishing their victory.

Happiness bubbled in us as we ate and played. Watermelon would appear and a platter of the juicy slices passed around would be gone by the end of the evening. Cantaloupe, too, and honeydew melon. We sat under the large mulberry tree in the shade and we kids went from one adult to the next, sitting on laps, showing flowers we'd picked, giving and receiving hugs and kisses. There was abundance in everything, there was exuberance, we were happy. For years and years, we were happy.

The adults worked six days a week — my father from at least 9 AM to 10 PM each day — so Sunday was a day of well-deserved rest. We went to Mass together Sunday morning, then changed out of our good clothes and gathered again to spend the afternoon and evening together outside in the nice weather. All summer long we picnicked, just like we spent afternoons together in the dining room the rest of the year. It was fun to be together, no one had anything to fight about.

In the evening, the lightning bugs would come out and we'd catch them in a jar, holding them there for a few minutes so everyone could have a close look, their light magic to us. No one knew a single thing about science, no one knew what made the lightning bugs light up. We all believed that God had made the world and every creature in it and we should take care of everything, enjoy and respect everything, and we did. We loved the lightning bugs.

We kids rode our bikes up and down the driveway, thrilled to go fast, and just as delighted to go slowly in curvy patterns back and forth, happy to ride, so happy to ride. To our delight, sometimes one of the adults would borrow a bike and join us up and down the driveway. Sometimes my mother would let us try to teach her to ride. That was hilarious to watch. She never did learn, but it didn't matter.

What mattered was that our gatherings were so enjoyable. We owned homes and looked after them, our backyards glorious with flower beds and vegetable gardens. Life was good. The sun could shine on us and we did not burn. Our history of stonemasonry and art bridged the ocean and painted the inside of our eyes. The sheep in Italy called us each by name. We saw the New World rooted in our ancestors' lives even as Grandma fingered her rosary beads. The warm summer sunshine smelled to us of home, smelled to us of Italy.

Dear Mr. Guiliano probably died of a heart attack while working in someone's backyard. I can see him reaching to trim a rosebush, exerting himself so that the yard he tended became a part of the Garden he saw in his mind, in his heart, a garden across the ocean, so that whenever he reached to trim a rosebush, he'd be reaching back home to Italy, back home to where my grandmother's prayers went, to where all the old people's thoughts and memories reached, while we children, growing without knowing, also grew by their hands, their prayers, their memories. They wrapped us in their embraces, they pointed for us to see, come look they would say, *bella, bella, como si bella*. And we, without knowing, became their children, learned to see what they saw, to taste life as they knew it, to smell the sweetness of their roses. We became Italian.

Reality Therapy

The chickens at the Italian Market lived close to the hospital. Straight and round Italian butchers greeted us with big friendly smiles, white aprons like the white coats of the doctors at the hospital. The chickens, also white, strutted and pecked in roomy wooden cages, murmuring softly as my mother carried me in, my head against her shoulder, still sleepy from the ether. One of the butchers, seeing me and the plaster cast on my legs, reached into a chicken cage to find a newly laid egg, still warm. He held it close to my face as if it were a jewel, and said it was for me to take home. Its perfect shape warmed my small hands and I smiled.

My mother smiled at him, at me, and asked him for a chicken, please.

The butcher looked over his plump chickens then turned to me to pick out one, pick out my favourite chicken, the one I liked the best. The rows and rows held so many fine ones, their fluff beautiful, their soft voices comforting. I pointed to one that was particularly fluffy and looked at the butcher. It would be nice to take that one home.

The butcher reached into the cage for my chicken, skillfully hooked its feet with one hand, brought it upside down screaming for its life to the chopping block, lifted the huge blade of the butcher knife high over his head, laid the chicken's head just so and chopped it off, draining the chicken's blood into a bucket adjacent to the block until the blood ran no more. He then moved the chicken across to the vat of boiling water on the other side of the block, the chicken sizzling steam as it was lowered into the boiling water. Soon all the feathers were off the fresh-killed chicken, and the bird was cut in eight for our family of seven, the neck and back wrapped separately, the liver and gizzards separate as well, the butcher smiling at me as my eyes grew permanently wider.

My mother cooked the chicken at home that night after using the burners on our gas stove to sear off the pinfeathers and after washing the chicken well in heavily salted water.

As I recall, the chicken was delicious. My mother loved the neck and gizzard best; I found the back most tender.

Schooled In Sainthood

In the 1950s, the Catholic school I attended taught us that our first goal in life was to become a saint. Absolutely nothing was as important as that. No one was encouraged to get a job of any kind once schooling was completed. No one was encouraged to pursue a career; that was immaterial. The status of the soul was paramount. If we felt "a calling" to the religious life, well, that was something we had to sort out with God and the nuns. We were never ever introduced to the want ads, to job skills, to practical training of any sort — in fact, the curriculum in those days didn't include science or physical education until grade five and little enough of it at that point. I remember Sister Mary Henry, my grade five teacher, skipping the first chapter in the science textbook (it dealt with the properties of light) because she herself didn't understand it. At that time, the world was a very different place than it is now.

My school, Saint Elizabeth of Hungary School, was a parochial school, which meant there was a church across the street. Because the church was so close, and maybe because it was exercise in lieu of physical education, our entire student body of Kindergarten to grade eight which, during the baby boom, was an astounding number of children, went to church more often then would be allowed today. I don't know how we got our studies done given the amount of time we spent on our knees in the church pews.

We went to Mass on Sundays, of course, that was required, but that didn't take away from school time. During school hours, we went to Mass on the first Friday of every month, every day during the forty days of Lent, and every day during the four weeks of Advent. We went to Mass every day during May and October, the months of Our Lady (after which we prayed the rosary), on the eight Holy Days of Obligation (none of which fell on Sunday), and we went to Mass of the feast days of special saints, like Saint Elizabeth, and Saint Joseph, of course. Our throats were blessed on the feast day of Saint Blaze. We got ashes on Ash Wednesday. We spent every Friday afternoon during the six weeks of Lent praying the Stations of the Cross, we went to the Novena of Our Lady every Tuesday afternoon, to confession every Friday afternoon, to choir practice, to prayers for peace, and to Benediction every Friday morning. We were encouraged to murmur what were called "ejaculations", which meant spontaneous short prayers like "Jesus, Mary, and Joseph, Pray For Us." Those were just the kind of thing to whittle away Purgatory time and we were encouraged to say them non-stop. Pray always, our teachers instructed us, and they were not kidding. Prayer was scheduled every day.

The rest of the school week we thought about prayers and said them at our desks as we sat quietly, incidentally doing math while pursuing our goal of sainthood.

From grade three on, we studied bible history, the Palmer method of Penmanship, and the saints. We had a book on the lives of the saints. Every day was a saint's day, meaning that some particular saint was in charge of that day, and we prayed special prayers to that saint, because we'd gain indulgences against our time in Purgatory.

Time in Purgatory was like time in the penitentiary here on Earth, it's time for crimes committed that aren't serious enough to warrant the death penalty, which in spiritual terms was Hell. Eventually everyone got out of Purgatory, but prayers could take days off your time, and since we were all told that we were sinners, always accumulating Purgatory time, we needed to pray. To "Pray always".

The nuns were keen to impart knowledge of the saints to us so we could be inspired to emulate the holy lives they led. The nuns would tell us which saint was good at what task, since each saint appears to have a specialty, like celebrities today who have certain causes they especially like. For example, Saint Anthony could help find lost articles because Saint Anthony knew where everything was. Lost and Found was his field of expertise. My Aunt Josie had a special devotion to Saint Anthony, and she prayed to him even when she hadn't lost anything. She just liked him. Because of that, anytime Aunt Josie prayed to Saint Anthony to help find something, it would turn up even if it wasn't Aunt Josie's thing. Saint Anthony did favours for Aunt Josie because she wasn't just a friend when she needed his heavenly help, she liked him for himself, and I guess saints rarely experience that.

So the nuns told us about the saints and their holy lives and the things they took care of — Saint Anthony, Patron Saint of Lost and Found; Saint Jude, Patron Saint of Impossible Causes; Saint Cecelia, Patron Saint of Music; Saint Sebastian, Patron Saint of Martyrs; Saint John the Baptist, Patron Saint of Lambs; and countless others. To further foster an appreciation of the saints, whenever we'd have a spelling bee in class, or if we did well on an assignment, the nuns would give us Holy Cards. Holy Cards were gloriously beautiful pictures of the saints, sometimes dramatic head shots of a tragic or ecstatic moment in the saint's life, but most often scenes of the saint doing something special, like Saint Francis, the Patron Saint of Animals, talking to the birds, the chipmunks, and the deer.

Printed on the back of most Holy Cards was a prayer to the saint and sometimes information about the saint such as their birth date, status as a martyr, if they were a virgin, etc., and we students collected these Holy Cards much the same as we collected baseball cards. Baseball cards were printed on cardboard, Holy Cards on high quality paper, often embossed, sometimes the edges gilded. They were heavenly.

I collected lots of Holy Cards because I was an exceptionally good speller, and an exceptionally good all-around student easily motivated by pretty pictures. I studied the beautiful cards, gazed upon them as we were taught to gaze upon holy things, prayed the prayers printed on the back, learned the various statuses and specialties of every saint I could, and dreamed of the day when I, too, would be successfully declared Saint Donna Marie, Patron Saint of something lovely. I didn't just want to earn my Eternity in Heaven, which was everybody's duty to do, I wanted to go that extra mile on the road to holiness and achieve sainthood. I wanted to be a saint, that was my goal.

And I was doing pretty well. Until, that is, one day a routine eye check in the school nurse's office resulted in my being sent to an eye doctor, who examined my eyes and declared I needed glasses. I was eight years old. I had started kindergarten early, at age four and a half, so I suppose I'd done considerable reading of Bible stories and prayers in the four years of schooling and maybe that's why I required glasses, I don't know. But I got my first glasses at that early age and have worn glasses ever since. Ordinarily, this would be an absolutely run of the mill experience, part of everyday life, but for me, really, nothing could have dealt a crueler blow. I've been devastated ever since, drifting, helplessly lost.

You see, when I saw myself wearing my first pair of glasses, I realized something was wrong. Soon enough I could name what it was. None of my Holy Card saints' pictures showed any of the Blessed Martyrs or Holy Virgins wearing glasses. They held their faces naked to Heaven, God had given them perfect vision. God had not granted me perfect vision, so I got the message — rejection by the Almighty, not chosen for the "A" team, sent back to the minors. I was hopelessly myopic, but the one thing I saw clearly was that sainthood wasn't in the cards for me. God didn't want me as a saint. There would be no Saint Donna Marie, Patron Saint of something lovely. No patron saint of anything at all.

Eventually I accepted the loss of my life's goal, and worked hard at living a vibrantly redemptive life, helping others, planning a life as a nun and serving the missions in China. Really. I attended a Catholic all-girls high school, where the nuns were fastidious in providing an excellent education for their students. The standards were high, they offered four full years of Latin, French, and Spanish, as well as progressive courses like Latin American History. The good nuns filled every single moment of the school day with a class of some sort, trying to eliminate free periods ironically known as "study halls", which were, in fact, scanty for studying and rife with opportunities for temptation. The nuns knew this, and if need be, would invent classes to fill up the schedules of their students.

One class in particular that the nuns devised became a real turning point in my life. We were given a choice (an unusual thing in those days), we could choose to take "Charm", where we would develop poise, good posture, good grooming, and where we would study appropriate feminine ways and manners such as putting on and taking off our gloves. The other course we could choose was "How To Survive a Nuclear Holocaust", which taught skills needed for life in a fallout shelter after a nuclear strike. It didn't take me long to decide. I chose "How To Survive a Nuclear Holocaust". While the Charm students were being weighed and measured and learning to walk and talk properly, I learned how to store food and water in a fallout shelter, how to arrange for a toilet in a fallout shelter, and how to deliver a baby in a fallout shelter. At the time, the Cold War was on and the skills I learned seemed absolutely and totally essential.

Regardless of the deficiencies in my charm quotient, I figured that in the end, knowing my way around a fallout shelter would prove more valuable than charm. Imagine my surprise when many years later, the Soviet Union came undone. Here I was, fallout shelter toilet skills intact and at the ready, fallout shelter food stocked and certified, the How To Deliver a Baby in a Fallout Shelter manual well-thumbed and nearly committed to memory word for word, and all this information now deemed useless, totally and completely, hopelessly useless, because the Cold War was totally over. The Berlin Wall came down, the Soviet Union split to bits, and I was obsolete. That was not my goal, ever. Given all this, in hindsight, Charm would have stood me in far better stead.

Past my prime, educated in an obsolete area, and not in the least charming, I found myself in the age of pop psychology, which I devoured religiously, as religiously as I'd devoured my Catholic formation. *I'm Okay, You're Okay*, self-help, it felt so *right*. Except for one very intrinsic part of pop psychology which advocated better life management by setting goals — long term goals and short term goals. *What do you want?* bald men with toothy smiles ask, *what do you want today, in a month, in a year's time?* Women in suits appear in infomercials, each word accentuated with a finger pointed at you as they ask the same questions. What are *your* goals?

I could never answer the questions pop psychologists ask. What do I want? How am I supposed to know that when I'm trained to do what God wants, what the church wants, what my parents want, what my husband wants, what my children want? There's not enough time to do anything else anyway after pleasing all those parties, so why waste time on wanting anything? My goals are to get through the day, period. That was how I've felt for years.

That is, until laser eye surgery came along, bringing with it a chance for me to entirely reconsider my life. Thanks to modern medical technology, I could spend a couple thousand dollars on a pretty safe operation which would permit me to fling my glasses away for good and do a U-turn. The heavens opened for me upon this realization, as astounding a turning point as my first pair of eyeglasses. Here, truly dawned a second chance. Should I do it? Should I forsake the fallout shelter for the operating theatre? Should I try again, perhaps to become Saint Donna Marie, Patron Saint of the Myopic? I relish the situation too much to decide. Do I want to be a saint, today, tomorrow, ten years from now? Or have I moved on to a new goal?

Life loves the circular, years revolve around seasons, planets spin the days around the sun, and life so often forgets to tell us we're not done yet. The cards — Holy, baseball, Tarot or whatever — have not all been played out. And the dreams we dreamed in olden days, enriched by the compost of life, can indeed rise up revived — aged and changed, but alive again nonetheless — to call forth hope beyond hope.

Confessions Of A Good Girl

As a Catholic student at Saint Elizabeth School in the 1950s, I learned about sin. I learned that sin is terribly wrong and makes us dirty inside, the illustration in our catechisms showed milk bottles spotted with dark patches to illustrate how gross sin was. Who'd drink dirty milk?

No one. Milk was always and only white in the days before chocolate milk, and seeing it spotted with dirt made it easy to see how gross sin was.

Luckily, we could go to confession anytime we wanted and that would make us white as the purest milk again with no dirty sinful smudges to worry about. That was terrific news. Even if confessions weren't until Friday, we could quietly speak to God and profess our sincere sorrow for our sins and they'd vanish in a snap. But we still had to confess to a priest first chance we got to make it official. The priest would give us a penance to say, usually three *Hail Marys* and three *Our Fathers* — prayers we said every day, and the nuns assured us that as we worked our way through the course of our penance, we would feel ourselves whiten and shine.

We made our first confessions when we were seven years old. The nuns explained what we might confess, and they gave us sample sins to consider, which was a good thing because I could never think of sins on my own. In fact, even after learning some of the sample sins, it was difficult to actually find a few that I had done.

Sister Mary Francis thought she gave a good example when she told us it was a sin to lie to our parents. Lie to my parents? The thought of lying to anyone much less my parents had never entered my mind as even a remote possibility. I didn't even understand what a lie was. Sister Mary Francis had to explain it to me. Lying, untruth, deception, I knew nothing of anything like that, and after I learned about it, lying seemed like a surprising and scary idea.

Sister Mary Francis also said it would be a sin to steal something, another activity I had never considered. She told us it was wrong to miss Mass, it was wrong to disobey my parents, it was wrong to eat meat on Fridays. What a revelation! Until she mentioned these activities I'd never conceived of anything so imaginative. Most of the other children felt exactly the same. We were innocent, the entire class; our only knowledge of sin came directly from God via Sister Mary Francis. Sin scared me, but in some ways it tantalized me, too. However, fear won out for quite a while and it was much later in life that I leapt into the abyss, overcame my fear, and tried a few sins on for size. But like I said, in my early years, I was content to contemplate sin safely from a distance.

We went to confession on Friday afternoons during the school year, as close to the obligatory Sunday Mass as we could get. The idea was to increase the chances of staying pure until then so that we could receive Holy Communion in the proper state of grace. If we sinned, come Sunday we would have to sit in the pew, embarrassed and exposed in our sinfulness, as everybody else passed over us to get to the Communion rail. The nuns would march us over to church after lunch on Friday, class by class, two by two, straight silent lines, no talking permitted.

Hushed, we entered the grandeur of the church, but even though we tiptoed quietly and dared not speak, we felt so very noisy in the vaulted marbled enormity of the sacred space of God's house, where every footfall was heard in Heaven, and even the murmurs of the nuns were just about audible.

The priest would enter the dark confessional booth, in many ways resembling a photo booth at the mall. He entered by the centre door, so that those going to confession could get into the curtained cubicles on either side to start their confessions. Once the sliding window to the priest's centre space opened, the "Bless me Father . . ." began, followed by the litanies of childhood sins. Of course, being in such close proximity to another penitent, we could, if we tried, hear what the other person was saying even if they were whispering. We all whispered, of course, because we were telling our sins and were ashamed. But we had been taught by Sister Mary Francis about this aspect of the Sacrament of Confession, this accidental hearing of another's sins. Priests were bound by a vow of silence regarding anything heard in the confidence of the confessional, and we, too, were as bound as the priest by the seal of the confessional, never to repeat under penalty of spiritual damnation any single little thing we heard that was part of another's confession. Sister Mary Francis said that we would burn in Hell if we did, and she certainly didn't lie even though she knew all about lies, so we became skilled over time at closing our ears so as not to hear, and holding our tongues about any sins that slipped through the confessional's curtains.

However, when Father Dominick arrived at our parish, everything changed. He had come to the priesthood via the army, leaving his post as a sergeant in his mid-thirties to join his God as a priest. One of the requirements of an army sergeant is a booming voice which, over long distances, can be heard very clearly. Father Dominick had that skill. He entered the church to hear confessions, vigorously waving us over to him like a traffic cop, his whackingly loud smoker's cough breaking like a gunshot into every meditative thought in the church, every prayer. Father Dominick threw on the stole of the confessional, which symbolized his authority granted by the church to hear confessions and to forgive sins, and broadly signaled for the kids to get into the confessional so the business of forgiving them could begin.

The door to his centre place closed loudly, he banged and rumbled as he sat and the normally silent sliding window that began the first confession slammed open abruptly. The children's voices were even more quiet than usual in fear of this big noisy fellow, and more than once he could be heard bellowing for them to speak up.

My experience with Father Dominick proved to be a breakthrough in my life. Until that time, I had taken advantage of the church's permission to confess previous sins as if they were current sins, sort of re-using sins, recycling on a spiritual scale, so that we could be doubly sorry for something we'd done. I wasn't actually sorry for anything that I'd done, but the church said I could be, and that meant I could confess a sin over and over as often as I wanted. Since I never sinned, I twisted every possible drop of badness out of anything I did that I might in some way be considered sinful. I had a couple of standard sins that I confessed, things like being late for Mass or disobeying my parents (when I stayed out to play two minutes later than I was supposed to), and those sins I confessed over and over. I just wasn't sinful enough to confess every Friday; maybe other kids were but not me. My life path ran cheek-to-cheek with God's.

I was glad to be done with confession at the best of times, and after confessing to Father Dominick I always felt drained and exhausted. His roughness embarrassed me, scared me, he was so unlike anyone else I knew, rumpled, gruff, and noisy. If one of the other parish priests had confessional duty, I hoped and prayed — even though it was a sin to do so — that I would get him instead of Father Dominick. *Mea culpa*, that was a real sin, and likely was why what happened, happened.

Father Dominick's confessional was particularly noisy one Friday, kids racing away from the curtained cubicles glad to be free, and when my turn came to enter I was more scared than usual. The murmurings of sins on the other side of the confessional were rather panicked, and I had to ignore an awful lot in order for my spirit to be properly penitent as Sister Mary Francis had instructed us, and when I heard Father Dominick boom out the Latin prayers of forgiveness for the child on the other side, I knew my turn was imminent.

And sure enough, the window with its opaque partition opened between Father Dominick and me, and I began as I'd been instructed, "Bless me, Father, for I have sinned, it has been one week since my last confession . . . " and then I listed the couple of sins as usual since I hadn't even remotely come close to sinning in earnest, and I awaited the priest's usual response, the issue of a penance, three Hail Marys and three Our Fathers and an invitation to make a good profession of sorrow for my sins by reciting The Confiteor, the standard prayer of penitence which meant I was sorry. But that didn't happen.

After my sins, Father Dominick bellowed, "Is that ALL?" I could hear the whole church go silent in response. "Didn't you do anything else?" He was really embarrassing me. I didn't know what to do. I had told him some sins, I hadn't committed any others, but I knew I had to please him because he was the priest and I had to get absolution because that's what everybody got from Confession. I could feel stress spiking my every heartbeat. Where could I find some more sins? Would it be okay to confess other kids' sins, adults' sins, feeling sorry on their behalf, was it okay to do that or was that a transgression of the sacrament?

I could feel his anger hot in expectation so I blurted out that I had lied to my teacher. He wanted more. I said I had eaten meat on Friday. "How much?" he asked, excited. "One bite," I replied, not wanting to appear too brazen in my disregard of the rules of the Church. Exasperated, he wanted more. I told him I stole jewelry. That seemed to make him happy.

He gave me the biggest penance I'd ever heard of, TEN Hail Marys *and* TEN Our Fathers, and then he allowed me to launch into The Confiteor. Afterwards he rumbled out the Latin prayers of Absolution.

It changed my life. The church had taught me many things, how to pray, all about Heaven, how to lead a good life doing what God wanted me to do, but Father Dominick taught me to sin, *required* that I lie. He required that I consider who made the rules, who broke the rules, and what was important to me. He made me take a step back and look at the big picture of what was happening to my soul. Father Dominick may not have known anything about grace, but he sure knew about salvation. And because he didn't do anything by rote, he made me sin so I'd have a real sin to confess, he made me taste my life and decide if it needed more meat, if it had enough salt, and if I should use a little less sugar.

SO FAR THIS LIFE

FIRE

MY FATHER ENVISIONED ME ONE MORNING AS he stepped out of the volcano.

He called to my mother in the forest and danced as he built a bed for them near a fire pit already warm with steamy rocks from the earth's very core.

His fire warmed my mother, making her cool waters steam like hot springs for my first misty cradling. He said to her, see this daughter of fire that I have made with you, her hair of flames, her eyes burnt with the night. My father branded me as his own forever. See the lines in palm and fingerprint that bear the mark of his people?

My father, born of the volcano, suckled my mother's breasts with sizzling tongue, with lips of flame, and warmed her mothering milk so that I was breast fed lava.

Doll Hospital

MARY, MY MOTHER, WAS THE BEAUTY IN her family. Together with her sisters, Josie and Angie, she left her sheep on the sunny hillsides in Italy and moved to New York, the most glamorous place on Earth. There, she worked in a beauty salon, bobbing hair and giving manicures, an easy segue for an artistic shepherdess. Josie worked as a seamstress in a dress factory, and Angie, the youngest, was a maid for a very wealthy woman who bought her things like hats in their own boxes, and hand-sewn gloves trimmed with fine black lace.

When I was little, I loved to watch my mother and her sisters. I watched them cook, and sew, shop, and laugh. They enjoyed everything from perming each other's hair, to working on the spaghetti supper for the church. I loved to watch them dress up, chatting and laughing in their smooth satin slips as they applied red lipstick to their smiling and generous lips. I especially loved to watch my mother. I savoured, delicately, with a single fingertip, the smoothness of her garters; I traced the line of her beaded bodice, up, around, and over her shoulder; I inhaled her every scent, from the moisturizer she put on her face, to her Lily of the Valley perfume.

Josie, the eldest, looked respectable and neat, always, even after serving supper to thirty relatives. Angie, the youngest, was always smiling, full of love. But my mother was the one with style; beaming, breathtaking, elegant. She subscribed to *Vogue* and *Glamour* and *Mademoiselle* She loved the way she looked, took care of the way she looked; taught us, her four girls, how to be beautiful. She, like a priestess, instructed us in the rituals of beautiful womanhood: filing nails, tweezing eyebrows, brushing hair, choosing clothing, walking and sitting properly. It was her passion, and our cherished destiny.

My sisters were better at it than I, as fascinated as I was by its every aspect. I walked like a duck, or so my mother would whisper to me as we walked to church on Sunday. Pick up your feet, she would say. I would try being more delicate, walking on my toes more. One foot in front of the other, she urged, instructing me, glad when I seemed to improve under her guidance, exasperated when my duck-ness persisted. My feet, like my father's, were EEE width; hers, AA. No wonder we walked differently. But I wanted to walk like her. I wanted to dress like her. I wanted my mother's womanliness so badly; I saw it flower in my older sisters, their posture, their carriage, their grace, and I wanted it myself.

My older sisters boarded away in high school. They attended finishing schools run by nuns; nuns who were graceful and ladylike, full of light and peacefulness; nuns who never got fancy with perfumes or strapless dresses. The nuns concealed their bodies, an exotic thing for a woman to do, I thought. There was something about it I liked; the secrecy, the enormity of the tiniest revelation, like the flash of wrist momentarily exposed. Women, concealed and revealed, a chocolate kiss in foil wrapping, the soft cream centre found when your tongue pierces and sucks the underside of a liquid centre cherry.

I wanted to be a nun, and I wanted to be a movie star, and I wanted to be a fairy princess. I would play with my stuffed animals, bears and dogs and bunnies, dressing them up in my mother's gilded scarves to be beautiful just like her, giving them voices and attitudes. My older sisters got real dolls to play with, because they were older and could take care of them. Dolls with porcelain faces and porcelain hands, with silk dresses, and soft hair you could really comb. My sisters, no one doubted, would grow up to be like their lovely dolls, while I, though we all fought against it, was well on my way to becoming a bear.

My mother stood in the sunlight by the kitchen sink wearing red heels and a red flared skirt under her apron. We brought her my sister's doll, broken after a bad fall, hoping that she could fix it. She turned from washing the salad greens in the sink to look, her bosom rising under her soft white blouse as she sighed, concerned. The doll's porcelain face had cracked, all the way from chin to eye, lending a hideous cast to the loveliness of only moments before.

The next day my mother took us all for a ride. I was in the backseat of the car when my mother pulled over and stopped in front of an old blue and white house, huge and rambling. She explained that it was the Doll Hospital. The very words surprised and chilled me. I had never imagined such a place, or such a concept, or much of anything about repairing broken things. Inside the Doll Hospital, shelves and shelves of beautiful dolls sat, waiting: some broken, some repaired — similar, sister-like, as if some tragedy had befallen an entire family. My sister's doll was admitted for surgery, and we left, glancing back at the Doll Hospital, comforted by the warmth and friendliness of the nurse who worked there, comforted by the atmosphere created by the many lovely dolls within, yet at the same time, anxious. We girls dropped off our shoes at Sam the shoemaker's shop for repairs, but dolls were precious possessions, never forgotten, never before left behind. Never never never.

A week later, no one was more relieved than I when we returned, picked up the doll, and brought her home. I would not have cared at all if she were as broken as before; I was just so glad to get her back with us again. The fact that she was fixed was a bonus, even though they had repainted her entire face to cover the repair, repainted it shades paler than she had been, as if the whole experience had left her drained, shaken. Changed forever, she came home with us, quiet as before, but with a new sadness that made her not quite herself.

I pretended to take my bears to the doll hospital to get broken arms or torn ears fixed. They would call out to me to please not leave them, but I would, hiding them behind the sofa cushions and walking away to watch my mother work in the kitchen. And later, when I picked them up, I pretended they couldn't smile anymore, even when I fed them cookies, and honey, and ham sandwiches. Their big brown bear eyes could only look to mine, unutterably sad.

It was amazing, when I look back on it, that my mother, with her dark brown eyes and black hair, her shortness, her plumpness, how she still managed to exude the sophistication and flair of the great women of the world, of actresses like Sophia Loren and Elizabeth Taylor, whom she admired; and fashion models, and queens. Her confidence in the power of her womanliness, the generosity of her womanly charms, the utter love she had of her sex, was marvelous. No barriers prohibited her enjoyment; she was convinced she was beautiful, and she was. Everything about her, every ounce of her, always, no matter what her age, what amount of silver in her hair, or what size her dress. I wish I had inherited her confidence along with her love of womanliness. Sometimes I wonder if things would have been different if I had.

There was no history of the disease in our family. There were none of the factors of predisposition present: quite the contrary, I menstruated early, had my first child early, breast fed him and his brother. Maybe it was something as intangible as a lack of confidence that left me susceptible. At any rate, I was twenty-nine years old when they cut off my first breast; thirty when they cut off the other.

ℰ ℰ ℰ

TUESDAYS WERE NOVENA DAYS WHEN I WAS in Saint Elizabeth School. Each afternoon the Dominican nuns in their white tunics and long black veils would walk us across the street to the church for the service to the Blessed Virgin Mary. The Novena was an opportunity to pray for something specific: in those days, we prayed for world peace, and for the conversion of Russia; we could pray for some special intention of our own as well, asking Mary, the Mother of God, to use her power on our behalf. I prayed that Joey would like me better than he liked Christine or Patti; I prayed that I would do well on my tests. Boys on the one side, girls on the other, we knelt in the silence demanded by the holiness of the place. The parish priest intoned the Litany of Holy Mary, and we responded over and over:
Mystic Rose
Pray for us
Star of the Sea
Pray for us
Morning Star
Pray for us
Queen of Angels
Pray for us
Throne of Wisdom
Pray for us

The afternoon sun shone down on us through the stained glass windows, making us sparkle like jewels, making us feel a part of the glory of Heaven and true children of the Mother of God:

Tower of Ivory
Pray for us
Queen of Peace
Pray for us
Mother of Divine Grace
Pray for us . . .

☙ ☙ ☙

TUESDAYS WERE ALSO THE DAYS THEY DID the breasts at the cancer clinic. Waiting for our check-ups, we sat in a small, crowded waiting room, on chipped old wooden chairs. We were not expecting to be comfortable, not when our minds were getting our affairs in order, deciding who gets what when we go. We were silent, all of us. It seemed appropriate, there being nothing really to say. My youth was apparent; some might have commented on that, but how? and why bother? We all knew what we knew. There was no sense pretending we didn't.

Once, an old Ukrainian woman came into the room, her first time there. She sat down next to me, her one arm swollen to twice its normal size. There was no silence for her. There was no silencing her. She turned to me, her voice ringing out in the quiet room like a gong. "They cut off my breast! Here! Look at my arm now, how swollen it is!" I looked; it was swollen worse than mine, probably because of her age. I looked at her, unable to speak. She cried out to me. "They cut off my breast! Those doctors!" There was agony in her voice. And mourning. "I'm eighty-two years old. I had a big garden. But now, they cut off my breast, and look what it did to my arm! Who can garden like this! She looked around the room and wailed to us all, "They cut off my breast!" Indeed, they had cut off ours, too. I wondered if we should intone it together.

They cut off our breasts
Pray for us
Who can garden like this
Pray for us
Mother of Divine Grace
Pray for us . . .

ౌ ౌ ౌ

My mother didn't garden, but my father did, and the pride of his garden were the roses he grew for my mother. She loved flowers of every kind, but especially red roses, especially his roses, fragrant and blood red and bountiful on the bushes in the long row he toiled over every summer. For an essentially practical man, he had an inordinate love of beauty. And the greatest beauty of all for him was my mother, whom he adored. He loved to delight her so that her eyes flashed and she smiled lovingly at him, which she did often, because he cared for her, looked after her, as his most beautiful rose of all. With ever more tenderness and appreciation as the years went by, he loved her, he found her beautiful, and she believed him, for she trusted him.

It was my father who answered when I phoned long distance to tell them about the cancer. My voice broke as I told him, and he got my mother, telling her something was wrong. Soon they were beside me, bringing me roses in the hospital, looking after my children. My mother shaved my legs and tweezed my eyebrows; she washed and brushed my hair. Everything was normal except my left breast and the nodes and other tissue near it had been cut off and thrown in a fire and burnt, and the rest of me went shopping for clothes that fit. Nothing fits a woman with one breast. I never even took off my coat, despite my mother's urging to try things on; all I wanted was to go home, to stay home, to never once leave home ever again.

In the hospital I had a nightmare. I looked in the mirror and saw my skull looking back at me, my teeth falling out, one by one. I awakened terrified. The first time I looked in the mirror for real, I was relieved to see my face and teeth intact, my hair on my head, my eyes in their sockets. But the pallor of my skin disturbed me, bringing back vague memories of long ago, of my sister's mended doll returning from the Doll Hospital, healed, yet so pale.

At least I was balanced after the other breast came off. Back at the clinic, young doctors accompanied the older ones on rounds, to learn more about cancer. I remember the first young doctor who examined me. Drawing down my gown from my shoulders, he touched my scars and asked, "Is it painful?" I wondered if this was what I would hear from now on from men who undressed me, not gasps of desire, or murmurs of appreciation, but dispassionate questions about pain, asked for purely scientific purposes.

As time went on, so did I. The cancer didn't reappear, my checkups at the clinic became annual, and after ten years, I was pronounced cured. More than a decade after the surgeries I learned that with my kind of cancer at my young age, I had only a fifteen percent chance of survival. I was surprised and pleased to have had such good luck without even knowing. But I still felt an incredible and overwhelming sadness about my body without breasts. More than a dozen years had gone by since I had worn a swimsuit, more than a dozen years since I had tried on new clothes in a store instead of ordering them out of a catalogue. More than a dozen years had gone by during which I dreaded and avoided telling every new friend, every new man, waiting for every reaction, every sidelong glance when they think I'm not looking. It's hard not to stare at a woman without breasts. The flatness under her clothing. It's a sight you seldom get to see. Curiosity, that's all, no harm meant, believe me, I understand. I found myself staring at women *with* breasts, trying to remember, what was it like? I had only fleeting memories of being whole. I was drawn to Picasso's work, amazed and embarrassed to see myself exposed in his paintings, jagged and split, fragmented, dispersed. Memories of my body before the surgery were far less real than memories much older, memories of my mother and her sisters, of my sisters and our dolls, of our excited preparation for the advent of our womanhood.

The day I started menstruating, I felt so shy about it, so shy and amazed that this bloody beginning, this becoming a woman, was actually happening to me. I was very scared of the enormity of it, of the task of knowing everything a woman had to know. I kept trying to find the right moment to tell my mother my news. She was busy cooking supper, pots steaming on the stove demanding her attention, the table being set, people in and out, the telephone ringing about the meeting she had to attend later that night. I wanted the time to be right. Private. So I waited and went to her in her room as she was getting dressed to go out. She smelled wonderful, looked wonderful as she stood in her slip before her vanity mirror, putting on her lipstick and her rouge. When I told her, she stopped right away and turned to me, her face bright with surprise and delight. She hugged me and kissed me as never before. Thrilled, she held my arms, looked at me in wonder, and hugged me some more. All the fears and apprehensions I had felt vanished. I could do this. I could do this act of becoming. I could go from caterpillar to butterfly, from bear to doll, from beast to beauty.

℘ ℘ ℘

There was a pantry in my mother's kitchen that I always loved. When I was little, I would stand in the doorway and look at the dark shelves, filled front to back and corner to corner with coffee and spices, anise stars, fennel seeds, virgin olive oil, all the essentials of Italian cooking. The aromas were as heady as my mother's scents — her perfume, the smell of her black velvet dresses, the lipstick she left on my cheek when she kissed me. And there was a glass sugar jar I loved to take down from the shelf and set on the windowsill, watching it shimmer and glint in the sunlight. My mother let me catch butterflies in it. They would light on the sugar when the lid was off, happy with this unconventional feast, content to let me watch them eat before they flew away to other, more normal, flowers.

℮ ℮ ℮

I didn't wear prostheses; it felt too reminiscent of pre-teens padding their bras. I was told the usual, that it wasn't important that I had lost a breast or two, that I was no less a woman for it. I tried my best to make it so. I was cheerier than I had ever been, handing out smiles as if they were free samples.

But facing cancer changes a person forever. Not only did I wonder if I would live or die, I questioned every aspect of every female ritual. Why bother with tweezing my eyebrows? Or shaving my underarms? Why wear jewelry? Or beautiful clothing? What was the purpose of these things? To attract men? Once attracted, then what? What man wanted a woman without breasts when there were so many with them?

As time went by, I became aware that I couldn't lead an uncharted life. I did not want to be always legitimizing, always disclosing, my alternative sex. When I looked at myself in the mirror, angry red scars where my breasts had been, I felt a growing and unrelenting sadness. Eventually, I understood that, while authoritative voices declared it wasn't important that I had lost my breasts, it was important to me. Important to me. I wanted to be fixed. I wanted my body to be familiar again.

Nothing would ever make me as I was before, but I needed to get as close to where I was so that I could begin to find my way again. I was lost, and I have a terrible sense of direction. Thankfully, my mother's inexhaustible love of being female had left a trail for me to follow, a trail that led me, fed me, saved me, helped me to find a way out of the darkness of being Venus disarmed.

Reconstructive surgery served, like my menstruation, as a second bloody ritual in my becoming a woman. Slowly my body began unfolding from its fearful state, coming to life again. I began to try on clothes in stores before I bought them; someday I hoped to swim. Memories of my mother and her sisters, of glorious days choosing clothes from overflowing closets, of sitting at my mother's vanity with her cosmetics and her jewelry box, abundant like her pantry. Those memories pulled me back, kept pulling me back, away from the fire where part of me had already gone, and into the goodness of ordinary, everyday, life.

❦ ❦ ❦

I SOMETIMES ASK ABOUT THE DOLL HOSPITAL. My sisters, as we all thought they would, grew to look even more beautiful than their dolls. My mother, as she grew older, grew more beautiful with each year. Neither she, nor her sisters, ever lost their vitality. And I began to find that when I looked in the mirror, I was reminded that I am of their line, not the spectre of my nightmare from the hospital. My body was no longer a puzzle. I, too, was a rose; bruised, but a rose nonetheless. It may have been my weakness that I needed all the parts before I could see that clearly, but what

I saw now comforted me. I was my mother's daughter, once again able to enjoy the womanliness she so loved.

When I went home, I would go to Saint Elizabeth's Church with my parents. My father would hold my mother's arm to help her up the stairs to go to Mass. And in the silence of the holy place, I felt deeply grateful for many things, but especially to my mother for her inexhaustible love of being female, and to my father, who appreciated her:

Mystic Rose
Pray for us
Star of the Sea
Pray for us
Morning Star
Pray for us
Queen of Angels
Pray for us
Throne of Wisdom
Pray for us
Tower of Ivory
Pray for us
Queen of Peace
Pray for us
Mother of Divine Grace
Pray for us . . .

WASPS

THE STROKE HAD SWITCHED OFF MY RIGHT side making it powerless, so when the wasps invaded the back bedroom in October a can of wasp spray became my constant weapon. If I'd swat at the wasps, I'd miss, or else the blow would be too weak to kill, only making them mad. With the wasp spray I could stand across the room and kill them, one drop of the stuff, even the fumes alone making the wasps fall from flight, protecting me from their stings.

They would arrive inside the house suddenly, in squadrons ready to attack, the sound of their buzzing an air raid siren day or night. The dilemma was whether to hold the pesticide can in my right hand or my left hand. Being right handed, it felt more natural to hold the can there, but the stroke had rendered my whole right side weak and spastic, uncontrollable, no longer the partner I could count on. When I closed my eyes and tried to touch the tip of my nose with my right hand, I'd miss, touch my chin, or my cheek, touch my lip, instead.

Although I felt connected to my left hand, we weren't much of a team. Even when I took piano lessons as a child, my left hand hadn't been strong. Forty years ago, my piano teacher bought a book of boogie-woogie for me just so I could develop my left hand. I managed to learn two pieces in the boogie-woogie book, not enough to help me out now.

The relationship between my right and left hands had changed since the stroke; my left hand really didn't know what my right hand was doing. Nobody did. My right hand, and indeed, my whole right side, had developed a mind of its own. I sometimes wondered who it listened to now. It must be rather nice to take off like that, to go away without notice, to not worry about responsibilities anymore. Surely my right side was enjoying this respite from the demands of life. I can see how tempting it is to just let go.

The wasps, sprayed with pesticide, twitched in their dying. With a tissue, I'd gather their bodies for disposal, carefully, for fear of being stung by a death spasm. The tingling in the fingertips on my right hand would intensify with the pressure of collecting the dying wasps — the tingle had become a constant sensation resulting from the strokes. It felt exactly like a wasp sting. They got me anyhow, I guess, those wasps. As if they were in my veins. It wouldn't have surprised me if they were.

In the hospital, when the doctors explored my veins for blockages that could cause a stroke, I'd heard the Doppler ultrasounds. There were no blockages, only roars in my blood every time I was asked to flex my feet, to move my body. All manner of monstrous creatures roared in my veins; monsters and oceans and time beyond this time. You'd think the sound of blood would be swoosh-swoosh, swoosh-swoosh, like water through a pump, but my blood roared louder than the ocean, louder than any lion, louder than King Kong. Blood roars so loud it's amazing that the world is so quiet. Whoever invented blood wanted to scream.

Hearing my blood roar changed my world-view so radically I desperately wanted to phone up Kierkegaard and tell him what I'd discovered. Or maybe Einstein or Hawking. Whoever invented blood invented a world made up of more than essential elements, a world of more than primary colours; whoever invented blood heard the liquidity of language, saw the mass and volume of dreams. Whoever invented blood built worlds within worlds, created a chaotic order out of mortar and pestle physics.

We are made of one hundred percent recycled material, formerly owned materials haunted by the former tenants, imbued with the archived hopes and cries of their hearts. It may be that in our flesh we house the compression of all the creatures who have inhabited our earthen selves, all the others who have used this earthy dust, the ashes to ashes, dust to dust of us.

Dinosaurs and palm trees and even Aunt Tessie can compress to oil and then to diamonds. Maybe we're on our way to being something hard and clear as diamonds. Maybe each individual lifetime in our cosmic matter is like a stitch on a sampler, a drop of seawater, an element in the grand and superbly bubbling physics of the universe. Who knows, maybe it takes all the bits of us — voice, thoughts, fears, everything, for planets or moons or asteroids to be formed. Maybe physics doesn't just include impersonal bits like neutrons and electrons, but whale songs and tail feathers and memories of school dances as well.

This disintegration of flesh and re-integration again must have gone on from forever, breaking down, rebuilding, breaking down, rebuilding, so that nothing that ever was is any longer the same, but re-formed into those who live now. Sabre-toothed tigers and mastodons are not extinct exactly, they live in the walls of my home, they migrate in the veins of my body.

But how can there ever be hope of knowing anything when we can't even hear on a day to day basis the shattering roars in our own blood? What if these wasps were not coming from inside the walls of my house, but from my bloodstream? And if that's the case, can it be that their energy is what once was mine? Can it be that this vacancy in my gut, this black hole endless depletion of sparkle that resulted from the strokes, could it be the wasps have it, now flaunt it blatantly, even in the record-breaking chill of this fall? If I let them sting me, would I get it back?

It had snowed, several inches. You would have thought the wasps would be quiet, would hibernate till spring. But something drew them in, made them want to see me.

People could have asked me how I was doing, if I could touch my nose yet with my right hand, but they could never imagine how foreign my right hand felt. I didn't even know if I wanted it touching my nose. Who knew where it had been, or what it had been doing. I certainly didn't. It was like having to rely on someone to take care of you. They can't tell if they're hurting you. They don't want what you want. My right side felt like a foreigner in my bed. An interloper. No help to me at all. An awkward silence.

There was a fence that had gone up along the centre of my body, like the imaginary line drawn to divide up the bedroom I shared with my younger sister growing up. She did what she wanted on her side of the room, things I would never dream of doing, played the accordion, put bows in her hair. My right side was like that: when a wasp came after me, my left side rushed to get away, but my right side stood dumbstruck, as if it didn't know what to expect. My left side, certain as to what to expect, was ready to flee. Or ready to fight. My right side, however, seemed ready to do a mind meld. Or maybe it was ready to die.

There were three strokes in all, on the right side, the left side, and at the back of my brain. The one on the left side took out the right side of my body. Maybe the one at the back of my brain was what made my speech slur, still makes my speech slur when I'm tired. Maybe the stroke on the right side of my brain affected me in ways I have yet to pinpoint. Maybe it was what made thinking so difficult. Maybe it was what made me so deeply tired.

Or maybe that was what impaired my tolerance. It fell to zero. One whiff of someone bullshitting and my agitation level would rise to bursting — people who pretended to be concerned about me, phone solicitors who called at suppertime ready to clean my furnace, shampoo my rug, ask for a donation to the Heart and Stroke Foundation. My patience vanished, too. And who knew what else.

In the night, I would wake up wanting to do calisthenics, desperate for sit-ups. My blood must have been disturbed by the stillness of sleep, the quiet in my veins, must have needed to roar. Or I would awake from dreams of running, my heart pumping hard in my chest, my face flushed. The running dreams were harder to understand. Was it the running itself that I long for, or the horizon?

When I was a girl, we lived above my father's store, and had to walk through the garages to get upstairs. Beer coolers were cleaned in the first garage by the staircase, and on warm summer days, the garage doors would be open, sunshine pouring in as my father and his workers rinsed out the coolers and beer kegs, sending warm sunny streams of beer and water running along the smooth cement floor to the drain over in the centre garage.

Large shiny black wasps, sometimes red wasps too, flew in to sip at the foamy streams. With their tiny waists and silky shine, those wasps seemed every bit as glamorous as my mother when she dressed in a strapless evening gown. Delicately, the fancy wasps flew above the beery waters, delicately they sipped just as I'd seen my mother sip from a stemmed crystal glass of crème de menthe over crushed ice. I wonder if the wasps would not have preferred champagne instead of beer. They seemed accustomed to a more genteel lifestyle. I remember them flying dreamily, legs hanging down as if they were carrying their purses. We were never bitten by those wasps. Not once.

The thick yellow and black wasps in the back bedroom's walls didn't look or act like the wasps of my girlhood. They emerged looking for trouble, flying anger, already roaring. Warmth and sunshine only made them madder. I wondered if beer would have mellowed them, but I didn't dare chance the outcome.

People here in town gave me advice all the time. It was my neighbours who suggested the beer. And the fellow at the hardware store who sold me the wasp bomb had lots of good advice about my wasps as well. In a small town, everyone knew about my stroke, and everyone knew about my wasps. It was as if the wasps had moved into the community, everyone observing them and making deductions as to what kind of neighbours they would be.

My house was made of wood. Wasps eat wood. And mine's a big house. These wasps must have been thinking they had won the lottery. I bet they were also thinking I'm the one who was the intruder. Maybe they were right. Maybe my right side didn't belong here anymore. I wondered if I could get half off on a ticket to send it somewhere warm.

It was cold. My right side was always cold. Ice cold. Ten degrees below zero and falling. Winter had set into my veins. I felt that soon my blood would turn white as snow, blue as ice. If you held my two hands, you would have felt the left one warm and the right one too cold to hold. What made my right side so cold? Had my spirit gone off somewhere? Would a picture of my right side appear on milk cartons?

The doctors told me it was important to rehabilitate the side affected by the stroke, to work the muscles so they could once again pump blood, pump it even when asleep. They needed to do it automatically, mindlessly, and mine had forgotten how. They needed a refresher course.

I would hold onto the wide back of an old chair and rise up on my toes. The muscles in my legs contracted, raising me upward into the grace I remembered of ballet dancers. I saw them in my mind's eye as I raised and lowered. Control and grace, tutus and leotards, tights and dancing slippers. My sisters danced and I watched. Even as a child, I was confined to the sidelines by some impairment or other. But in my memory, the dancers danced for me forever, and helped me reprogram my imagination to the discipline of ballet.

First position, you place the feet so, raise up on toes, hold the head high, shoulders back and down, soft but strong. My mind, so muddled from the strokes, and so unable to remember what day it was, or remember what groceries I needed, or whether or not I had taken my medication, could remember the ballet barre exercises with ease.

How could this ballet memory and the memory of the ancient ones who roar in my blood be so long and clear? Memory of the present time was not clear. The strokes had erased it. What was I doing, what was I supposed to buy, what thought did I just think, who was it I was speaking to on the phone, questions my mind repeated and repeated. But with the ballet, my muscles felt extension, felt controlled movement. I remembered seeing it in my sisters, who still danced for me in my memory, forgetting they are fifty or sixty, and their dancing enlivened my silent limbs, as graceful as the flight of the delicate wasps in my father's garage.

Twenty degrees below, colder with the wind chill, colder yet for my right side. The memory of summer warmth, the memory of dancers, those memories acted as a warming wind to fight the winter chill, to pull my right side along, back into step, back into line, back into rhythm. A reluctant dancing partner, it preferred the stillness of the shadows, but there were undeniable pathways connecting us.

Herds migrated in my veins, flocks of birds fluttered up into a blue endless sky, and troops of ballerinas jeté'd on point. The buffalo stampeded from my left side through my right, snorting, heads down, hooves high. Herds on every continent throughout all time howled in my blood. Even the ballerinas roared in my memory. The wasps would not let me alone. Even in the cold quiet of November, slower and no longer able to fly, they crawled to me to whisper their ancient buzz.

Once alive, it is impossible to die, life recycles eternally. My right side dreamt of death which could not be. It may as well return to me for now, if not a marriage of love, then one of convenience. Time passes and we go on to become a thousand other things. Right now, we just have to get through this life.

My Personals

An elaboration on an ad

SWF, 50, seeks male: intelligent, passionate, good sense of humour.

S

    SWF, 50, seeks male: intelligent, passionate, good sense of humour.

    Single? Well, not married anymore. Some say divorced, but to me that means you still have feelings. Of course I have feelings, I just don't feel married anymore. I don't even feel divorced anymore. I'm single. One plate. One pork chop. Single.

W

    SWF, 50, seeks male: intelligent, passionate, good sense of humour.

    White. Is Italian white? Southern Italian? Mountaintop Italian from peasant stock, with olive skin that never ever sunburns, with eyes as dark as the inside of a cave? Look at me and tell me what colour I really am. When you read my ad and then you see me for real, will you be thinking, *White?* No way. I look in the mirror, there's no white woman there. I'm brown; or green; as brown as the earth, as green as the olives. My blood is a mixture of red wine and olive oil, of hazelnut liqueur and marinara sauce. Leaves fold against my face and along my eyelids; grapes sprout in my hair and the sighs of my dark-eyed aunts nestle along the inside of my thighs. You could describe me any number of ways, but white? No, never.

F

SWF, 50, seeks male: intelligent, passionate, good sense of humour.
Female. But when you say female, what image do you have? Is it me? Hardly likely. I don't think I've ever painted my toenails. No one's ever called me petite. I'm not cute. Nor sweet. My sideways glance though, sizzles. Men find me attractive. Exotic. I think making love to me must be like making love to a mythological creature, half-human, half-beast. A fecund mixture of earth and fur and sweat; the fiery belly of Hell itself. Come, explore my depths; you'll hear the wild things breathe. Unfold me and you slip through the ages into airy shadows, into slow and succulent wonders. Sweet things, too. The grace of antiquity. Feel the lion and the bird; hear the song of a thousand souls. I'm not modern. No. Not kitchy. Not me. Not *Baywatch*. No *Playboy* spread. But in my eyes, in steamy darkened shafts of golden light a Goddess lives, and a bear. Their faces, two-faced; my face. Kiss me and you kiss a Goddess; kiss me again and you kiss a bear. Astonishing how loving this bear-goddess can be.

Beware the danger you so love. I come with a warning: proceed at your own peril. Prepare yourself to be disarmed. Your walls will crumble, your barricades melt leaving your heart defenseless, aglow with the warmth of safety and the thrill of adventure. You'll meet my lovers along the way: Marco Polo, Saint John the Baptist, Groucho Marx, Nebuchadnezzar; a Bengal Tiger, a gorilla, a swan. Prepare yourself for heaving aside rocks from sepulchers, for discerning the writing of the ancients. I will let you in, and I will block no path, and I will do no harm. But in this new world, who will you be? And what of yourself will you discover?

50

SWF, 50, seeks male: intelligent, passionate, good sense of humour.

A story fifty years long. Does that interest you? And you, will there be moments and threads and eras you'll want me to know about? Or with this ad, are you looking for just a throw-away, another lapsed Catholic moment, where nothing significant happens, no one reaches into anyone's innards bare-handed to examine intimately, to hold and extract, to attempt miracles. If I were a vending machine, would that be just as good? Do you want to know about my grandfather's stone barbecue where he built charcoal fires that blackened succulent steaks? Do you want to hear about the delicious gracefulness of Grandpa's screened-in arbor where my parents sat with us their five children, sat in the early evening under the shade of Grandpa's grape vines and ate that charcoal-broiled steak along with salad from his bountiful garden, a jug of his homemade wine as always at his feet, a glass for each of us, even the toddlers? Grandpa's house in summertime; the memory always makes me smile, always makes the demons in me quiet.

There are more stories: Uncle Nick and his sidekick, Rocky; Aunt Josie's homemade ravioli; olive groves on Italian hillsides and Uncle Alberto's gourmet nut kingdom. I lied when I said my story was fifty years old; it's from forever. My mother's father grew up in a cave; to understand that one thing alone will take a lifetime. And their stories are mine. It's a ball of string inside me like those toys where you point the arrow and pull the string and a voice speaks. You ask about me, I talk about them, you learn about me. How many faces do you see? How many angels dancing?

SEEKS

SWF, 50, seeks male: intelligent, passionate, good sense of humour.

Sometimes seeks, not always; not pathologically. Seeks as an Arab seeks the horizon, seeing it always just ahead, content in the sandy path undulating underfoot, without knowledge of pavement or longing for highways untravelled. Seeks sometimes as a loosened veil seeks the floor. Seeks sometimes as the wind seeks the next rustling of leaves. Seeks sometimes as a warm, moist, mouth seeks the sweet cherry's solid pit.

MALE

SWF, 50, seeks male: intelligent, passionate, good sense of humour.

The warm male smell. I breathe it in and a deep calm settles over my every pore like a soothing balm, the sweetest lullaby, a garden close to God's own heart. I've never met I man I didn't like to smell. Scratch the surface and you smell earth and vines and sweat and books and oil and tweeds and ancestors come from a far-off land. Explore and you find treasures, mysteries and truths held together with a strength that smells distinctly and richly male. Here, the fears conquered daily. Here, the white coals of passion. Here, sweet tenderness. Oh, that tenderness, smelling the most seductive of anything on earth to me. A loving male surely is the smell of Heaven itself. Some women love aftershave, sure, that's fine. Some love tuxedos, some fresh-washed jeans, some ballet tights. Me, too. But more, I love more. All you have to do is show up warm and alive and let me smell you and I'll smile with contentment.

As for looks, yes, I have preferences. Rocks and frogs and earth, faces of colour and texture and honour, courageous faces not pretty but gritty, oozing culture and sizable spirit, formidable interiors, vast halls and secret passageways. I might not hold it against you if you're handsome, but I've never loved a handsome man easily. Handsomeness doesn't attract me, other qualities do — quality men, not handsome men. Men whose character chisels itself boldly in their eyes, their mouths, and the set of their shoulders. Men who love women. Respectful, graceful, men. Strong in themselves, their strength easy, easing, accommodating. Men whose strength is a pleasure to behold, soft and generous. Men who love with their whole being, whose testosterone makes them lovely flowering trees, and nesting eagles, and dancing northern lights. The men in my family were like that: Nick and Rocky, my father, my grandfather; their tough hands tenderly holding a buttercup to make me smile.

INTELLIGENT

SWF, 50, seeks male: intelligent, passionate, good sense of humour.

On the prairie the horizon is endless; ranging. A mind like that; like the prairie; open, seeing, looking close, yes, but also far far away, loving the expanse. The breathing mind. At home on the verandah. The dancing mind, the singing mind, the quiet listening mind. I don't care what your interests are; I care about your gaze, then your focus, your interior mirrors, your weaving of story and scope and mystery and science. There's room for me, then, with a man of like mind.

PASSIONATE

SWF, 50, seeks male: intelligent, passionate, good sense of humour.

A man who can give his heart. He knows its value and vulnerability, but can still give his heart; desires to give his heart, knows who to trust with his heart, and the consequences of trust and love. A sensual man who can sway with the pulsing of the universe, receiving as well as giving, tasting the richness of life, knowing where to focus to get the best view, luxuriating in the abundance of the greens and blues, the smiling yellows of this world. Whose reds deepen to purple; whose clear eyes sparkle when we meet and speak and argue and make up. A liquid-centre man, a pool, a stream, an ocean of a man. A man who sometimes can't resist the moon, who sometimes must shape wood till its edges smooth; a man who inhales hard to smell the.world, inhales so deeply his eyes shut tight.

GOOD SENSE OF HUMOUR

SWF, 50, seeks male: intelligent, passionate, good sense of humour.

Laughter tickles us from the inside and makes us glow; intimate yet most respectable. I love the closeness that humour brings, the gears that mesh, the sweet safety of the bumper cars in our minds. We can feed on each other's insights and bend and shape the world as we bound from subject to subject, so in tune anyone could tell we came from the same planet. I'll enjoy you thoroughly. Our time together will be unforgettable. Brilliance, gloriosity, and small whispered questions — oh, the sweetest seduction! We'll be at home within each other, our memories full of delightful sparkle and comforting warmth. Recreation at no one's expense. Free-ranging, playful, classy, smart, from-the-heart sense of humour. No puns, please; well, maybe once a year if they're really good.

❦ ❦ ❦

THERE WILL BE A PAUSE HERE IF *you've come this far. The ad is over, and you must decide if you want more and at what cost. Risk circles you on every side, as inevitable as a tax. Should you choose to leave now with certitude, then good for you; what you want is elsewhere. Should you leave because of shyness, then I wish you wouldn't. Would I could only spin a screen of honeyed silk so you could look into my eyes, and feel my touch before you had to decide to stay or go, before commitment to walking one more step.*

Maybe there is just too much fear to conquer today and it is best to walk away before disappointment strips off one more veil of hope. The likelihood of us finding each other through any means, this or otherwise, diminishes every day. The likelihood of finding happiness may have always been a myth perpetrated by those selling flowers and chocolates and candlelight dinners, baby cribs, insurance policies, and Caribbean cruises. Perhaps the promise from these writings is enough for you. Perhaps it is all your heart can bear right now.

Know this though: At this point, I have not rejected you nor you me. But like the "Ode On a Grecian Urn", we have bent towards each other in a kiss that has neither begun nor ended but lives in hope forever. The choice is always to let this kiss-wishing be the history, or to let the kisses come and go, slipping onto the conveyor belt of time for processing and packaging later.

Whichever our choice, the sun defines each day, hour by hour, its rainbow-light sparkling. Those rainbows bathe us, penetrate us, urge us skyward towards the sun that, as Icarus found, warms us wonderfully yet burns us up when we get too close. But retreating entirely from the sun kills us just as surely. There is a balance then that we need, a perspective we must discover. Like clustered sun dogs, we must find the safe distance, the perfect place to sit where we can arc the light from one to the other, to make a rainbow visible across the sky.

I have yet to do that.

Have you ever?

I Believe

THE MID-SUMMER SUN SHONE BRIGHTLY THE DAY my mother took my younger sister, Carol, and me into the living room for a talk. It was a novel experience for us at our tender ages. Every other time my mother wanted to talk to us she'd start with a loud call from another room naming each of her children starting with the eldest and descending down the list until she got to the one she intended to send to the store, usually me, the fourth.

"Cookie, Paul, Micki, Donna . . . !" she would call out, as if she were in Church, petitioning the saints for help in some crisis. I think it was the only way she could remember my name. She had wanted three children and I was the fourth, so she struggled with fitting my existence into the plan she had prepared for her life, and she had to scroll down the list until she came to me, Donna Marie, named for my father and my mother, intended to be their absolutely last child. The fifth child, Carol, surprised my parents again when she came along less than two years later. We were born in the days before family planning, or rather when family planning meant crossing out the old plan when a new child came along and re-ordering the future according to the revised plan.

So my mother's call to Carol and me to come into the living room because she wanted to talk to us made us wonder if something was wrong. We were Catholic, raised when Catholic children went to Catholic schools. We were completely innocent of any wrongdoing, happy to do whatever was expected of us, happy to be compliant, never giving a thought to being bad in action or temperament, yet we had learned about sin and evil in school, the nuns carefully teaching us about such things as the devil, mortal and venial sins, commandments, church rules, and, like good Catholic children of the time, we both had learned to cringe with guilt with every breath, trying not to do anything wrong but always conscious of doing every single little thing wrong, praying every day, day and night, going to Confession every week, apologizing to God, the angels and saints, apologizing to everyone, sorry, sorry, heartily sorry, prayers about being sorry memorized and ready to say by heart just in case we were close to death and needed a prayer of atonement to squeak us through the pearly gates. Guilt, our first solid food, fed to us with our mother's milk.

So, again, my mother wanted to talk to Carol and me and she sat us side by side on the sofa in the living room, right next to the fireplace, and she herself sat across from us, her knees nearly touching ours. Her face looked both happy and sad as she readied herself. I could see she had considered this for a long time. What would she say? Was she sending us away, was she going away herself? I was nine and Carol was seven, all we could understand was home and family. And God, we understood God because he was part of the family; and we understood angels and saints — with all the statues and pictures of angels and saints in our homes we felt they were part of the family, too. Certainly we'd heard enough about them from Aunt Josie who seemed to know them all better than anyone and who loved them so much it made her cry just to think of them. And at school the nuns taught us about the saints; in church, too, we named the saints and prayed every day to at least one of them, their intercession on our behalf invoked daily. Our names linked us to a particular saint to obligate that saint to look after us, just as parents or sisters and brothers would.

At school we knew about angels because from day one we learned that our guardian angels got tired flying over us and we needed always to make room for them on our desk seats. Angels and saints perched, hovered, listened always. That was why the nuns and priests trained us in prayer: angels and saints listened, did we talk to them or just ignore them? It wasn't polite to ignore angels or saints any more than it was to ignore people, so, we had to pray.

If my mother wanted to tell us about anything else other than home and family which included God, angels, and saints, we couldn't imagine it. Home and family were everything to us. So if she had something to say, it had to be very important. And it was.

She told us in a soft, half-smiling way, that we were getting older and there was something we should know. Carol and I sat silent as stones, our eyes wide and unblinking, in wait for what we knew would be important information. My mother told us there was no Santa Claus. She and our father bought the Christmas presents and set them out for us, not Santa. Santa wasn't real.

Both Carol and I must have looked shocked. Carol was angry as Carol is wont to get when dreams are shattered. I, so typically, shuffled through the files in my brain to find a counter-story to combat my mother's claim. I was in deep conflict. Certainly I didn't want to contradict my mother outright, but how could I have been so wrong all my life about something as fundamental as Santa Claus? My mother may as well have told me there were no angels, no saints, no God.

But she had spoken, and she wasn't saying, "Go to the store for me", "Bring this dress to Aunt Josie to hem," or "Set the table, it's time to eat." She was telling us there was no Santa Claus. No Santa Claus? I had seen him myself, so had Carol. But my mother said those were just helpers, other adults who wanted little kids to believe. There was a conspiracy, apparently, of perfectly respectable-looking, church-going adults, who lied to children to perpetrate the idea that there was a Santa Claus — who apparently was a phantom that didn't really exist on any plane of existence, not even in Heaven, not even in Purgatory, not in Limbo, not even in Hell. I couldn't believe it. Adults didn't do things like that. What had happened to my mother? What made her lie about Santa?

Carol and I struggled with the revelation that had come this sunny afternoon from Mary, our mother, in our living room. We both knew that revelations came to children elsewhere, we had learned about them in school. For example, Mary, Mother of God, had appeared to Bernadette, a shepherdess. Mary was in a tree on a hillside, and she gave young Bernadette a secret message. Mary, Mother of God, seemed quite fond of appearing to children all over the world, not just at Lourdes, but Guadalupe, Fatima, Paris, Rome. My mother Mary was just the mother of us, not God, but why had she chosen to reveal this message to us? Was she confused? Misinformed?

"It's more fun to believe, isn't it?" she said understandingly, at last sounding like our real mother instead of this Santa-denying wicked witch. Then suddenly I recalled an experience where, from my bedroom down the hall, I had heard the rustling of the Easter Bunny setting out baskets of chocolate goodies for us all. While I had not actually seen the Bunny, I heard him, no doubt in my mind. It was not a dream, I was certain. I had heard the

Bunny, and I was heartened by this rather close encounter and spoke up, eager to salvage some scrap of the Santa fantasy.

"Maybe", I said, "there is no Santa Claus, but I know there's an Easter Bunny because I heard him; I heard him myself."

My mother looked at me, considering what to say. She sighed and smiled, deciding not to pulverize my wisdom about how the world works. I was a believer, and she would not convert me to reality any time soon. The Bunny stayed.

Eventually, as I grew older, the Easter Bunny and Santa became equals in my mind with angels and saints. Sure, parents, family, and friends bought presents at Christmastime and chocolates at Eastertime, but the spirits of generosity which looked after us all in the darkest time of the year, and in the new spring season, remained as real to me as the angels and saints, which no one doubted.

My mother never tried to speak to Carol and me again in the way she had that day. She must have realized we were hopelessly converted to believing in things, all things, any things. And no matter what adults were doing to eradicate the stardust from other kids, we were adamantly holding onto ours.

Easter Bonnets

Jackie Kennedy boosted the hat industry but my mother did her part, too. It all started with my Uncle Alberto, my mother's only living brother. He had lots of children and a very dear and loving wife, Aunt Christina. Uncle Alberto worked in a box factory making fancy hat boxes, and because he was poor, he gave these fancy hat boxes that he made himself as presents to my mother and her sisters. When he visited at Christmastime, Eastertime, Mother's Day, Uncle Alberto brought hatboxes. They were beautiful, and of course, my mother wanted to fill them with hats.

Since she had four daughters, along with my grandmother who lived with us, and herself, my mother had six heads to cover with hats. This was at the time when the Catholic Church required under pain of sin that every woman's head be covered when in church. We committed sins in private, not in full view of anyone, especially not our congregation, our nuns, and our priests, so no woman went into church without her head covered by a hat, or a mantilla (veils we carried in our purses), and if caught unawares by a surprise visit to a church, then a plastic rain hat, a hankie, or Kleenex would have to do. But the uncovered head never was seen in church, so it was a time when women had hats. Lots of hats.

Easter hats in particular. All year long we attended church services at least once a week, sometimes every day, our heads covered always. And because of Judy Garland's movie, *Easter Parade*, Easter became my mother's favourite time for hat buying. Usually she bought us hats in the hat section of large department stores, but when she learned about a real hat store in a nearby city, she took me with her to buy our Easter hats there.

The shop was full of fine hats: feathers sweeping down and to the side, or perky feathers standing up and pointing to the sky. Straw hats, cloth hats, cloche hats, small hats, veils for elegance, veils for mystery, mourning hats, broad-brimmed hats, sun hats, evening hats, ladies' hats, girls' hats, nothing but hats. And if you didn't see one you liked, there was a man there, the hat maker, who would whip one up for you as easily as if he were making an ice cream sundae. That's what he did for me.

I was thirteen, newly initiated into the rites of womanhood, and my mother gave me a yellow spring coat, quite special because it was my first coat bought for me, not a hand-me-down from my older sisters. That Easter I was to wear my first bra, my new Easter dress, my new yellow spring coat, new high-heeled shoes, a garter belt, stockings, and a new hat, the one the hat maker would make for me.

The hat base was white straw, a round inverted saucer on top of my dark hair. To that base, the hat maker attached a veil of yellowish-white net, the kind a girl would wear for daytime going-to-church occasions. Onto the netting, he sewed individual white and yellow daisies, sweetly scattered as if newly fallen from the sky. He fashioned this lovely hat in minutes, looking from the hat into my eyes, to see if he was getting it right.

He did indeed. Every Easter since that Easter, I've remembered that hat as my ritual entry into womanhood. My first spring as a woman, my first ceremonial head covering. I wore it for years afterwards, even after it wasn't necessary to wear hats in church anymore.

Through the white veil on my Easter hat that encircled my face and hair, I saw the world differently, no longer a child, but maturing in body and spirit into the woman I was to become. At other springtimes, I would wear graduation caps to celebrate personal accomplishments; when I married in spring, I wore daisies in my hair. The root of all these head coverings: the hat maker's Daisy hat. He saw it in my eyes, the hat that belonged to my life, the sweetness that spring brought.

My mother had many hats, her womanhood more complex than almost any woman I have ever met in my whole life. My womanliness paled in comparison to hers. I had a simpler head, and a more simple life. For her, roses; for me, daisies. Not just for our hats, but in our hearts as well. The hat maker's creation made me see the beauty of simplicity, and set me off at a young age down a path uncomplicated and sure, one I could walk securely, even in high-heels.

Black and White Time

THE WARTIME BLACK AND WHITE NEWSREEL FOOTAGE shown in North American theatres made the world look as if colour had been yet another casualty of war. As if all robust cheeks had taken on the pallor of death; and as if even the civilians, safe in their homes an ocean away from war's guns and trenches, had grown weak, unable to bear the brightness of colour.

But not my mother. At a time that every new house had walls painted white, my mother had deep eggplant-purple walls in the living room of our new home over the store. With a silver-grey rug, it was very daring, rich and luxurious. Vibrant house interiors were rare; white felt tranquil and clean at a time when the world was dusty with rubble, exhausted from the war, and too tired for colour.

But my mother always had to have colour, she loved colour, especially red: red lipstick, red nail polish, red clothes, red shoes. It's her colour. And it's the colour of Christmas when red appears everywhere, so Christmastime for my mother was a truly happy time.

Since there were five children in our family and my mother liked to dress us alike as much as possible, Christmas presented the perfect opportunity to get us our yearly pair of pajamas — red pajamas. She glowed as she posed with us for Christmas pictures every year in our new red Christmas pajamas.

We girls didn't get to wear colours very much otherwise — we wore navy blue jumpers and white blouses for our school uniforms; my brother and my father wore dark pants and white shirts every day. It was the 1950s, black and white was everywhere, in movies, in photos, on TV, even the Dominican nuns who taught us at school wore long black veils and long white tunics.

Household appliances were all white, no avocado green, no gold, no chrome until years later. Washing machines, mix masters, all appliances were white, the only choice at that time. We had a washing machine to do the laundry, a Maytag which did a very good job cleaning our clothes, and that was, of course, white as well.

My mother would use bleach on the whites, so that the whites got really white. On TV, detergents like Tide would encourage women to get whiter whites, to be proud of how white their whites were when hung out on the clothesline. Sheets, pillow cases, shirts, blouses, undershirts, slips, bras, underwear, whatever was white needed bleach to make it gleam on the line. Washing and whitening went hand in hand.

So we washed our whites with bleach, and we hung them on the line, even in winter. We did the laundry every Monday. The dark and coloured clothes separated to be washed later, my mother would put in the white clothes, the detergent, and the bleach, close the lid, and listen to the Maytag spinning, shaking, and sighing until the wash was done. Then, the lid would be lifted and the wet clean clothes removed to either the clothesline or the ironing board.

But not all went as planned. Inevitably, some months after Christmas, when we all were used to our new red pajamas, someone's red pajama top or bottoms, (the littler ones from me or my younger sister) would accidentally wind up in the load of white blouses and shirts. Everything formerly white was pink from that day forward. Pink school uniform blouses, pink shirts for my father and brother.

Pink was not a colour for men back then, and my father couldn't stand in front of his customers wearing a pink shirt. It wasn't done. In fact, the red pajamas dying the white wash became such an awful, predictable, yearly disaster that eventually my father had his shirts done at the laundry service instead of in our home.

My mother would try to bleach out the pink so that my brother and us girls wouldn't run into trouble with the nuns at school. The school uniform was white not pink, and the black and white nuns would not allow pink to replace white for anyone.

The first time this happened, I was shocked. I was embarrassed. Going to school in a pink uniform blouse and having to explain to everyone what had happened mortified me. I felt like a failure not being able to have the right colour blouse, the colour that everybody else seemed perfectly capable of having throughout the whole year.

But over time, the pink wash became part of our family's ritual of spring, the pink shirts a signal of the end of wintertime. The white snow gone, the tulips bursting through warm soil, the white uniform shirts and blouses, too, blossomed like flowers, pink and pretty.

Eventually, the world got more of its colour back. After the wars, people all over had become a little pale, too much blood lost, too much of everything lost. But in time, colour returned, and the pink uniform blouses and shirts weren't such a disaster anymore. My mother's love of red remained, and I often wonder if that persistent red of hers which endured at a time when interiors of houses were white as a bloodless corpse, I wonder if that red of hers wasn't like brandy to a sick person, reviving and healing, helping to bring the roses back to our cheeks.

Journey Without A Map

My mother was born after the twin boys died. Influenza ravaged the world, and my grandmother, Michelina, looked after her eighteen-month-old twin boys, as well as two older children all by herself in Italy, her foolish husband away in the New World dreaming of a new life for them. When the priest entered the house, he found my grandmother and the twins lying in the bed, the twin boys dead, my grandmother nearly dead between them with an arm around each. The priest said he could smell death on her breath.

He poured wine down her throat and prayed. It revived her. She buried the twins in the village graveyard, cursing her absent husband as she prayed for the souls of her sons. Her husband, Vincenzo, would return by boat across the ocean from the New World too late to help her, so sorry for the loss of their sons, and eager to console his Michelina with more children.

She gave birth to my mother after the loss of the twins. My grandmother and my mother both learned a lot from that experience: my grandmother learned that a woman always forgives the man she loves no matter what he does to her, and my mother learned that life is about living, not dying, not ever about dying.

I don't think my grandmother and my mother ever got along well. Proud and strong-willed, they loved each other, but they were rivals, too. My grandmother loved her husband, Vincenzo; my mother loved her father, Vincenzo; but they loved him for different reasons, and each hated what the other loved in him.

Vincenzo, was a tender man, sweet as a butterfly, and Michelina loved that about him. But he wanted Michelina to come to the New World, to give up the farm and follow him, trust him, believe him that she would love life in the world he had discovered across the ocean. But she refused. She wouldn't. Her land had belonged to her family. She loved it and she couldn't abandon it: not the horses, not the sheep, not the fields, not the nut trees, not the olives. Her family was buried here. Her children belonged here. If she had followed Vincenzo, where would they be? Who would they be? He had talked of leaving Italy since they were first wed. If she had listened to him as he suggested a good wife should listen to her husband, her children would have been born in the New World, not in Italy. Ironically, my mother would have been happy had that happened.

My mother missed her father when he was away from the family. She wanted to be with him. And she desperately wanted to experience everything he told her about the New World, the glorious things, the shiny things, the city life of opera and shops. She wanted him to insist that her mother come with him, hated that he was so soft towards her, so loving.

My mother had listened to her father talk about clothing shops in the New World where clothes were already made, not hand made like the white clothes they made from the sheep wool here in Italy at the farm. New World clothing with colourful fabrics and beautiful buttons, made in factories, hanging in shops for girls to come and choose their favourite dress, their favourite scarf, their favourite skirts and sweaters. The ideas of such glorious clothing bedazzled my mother when she was a young girl, colours and fabrics swimming in her head like fields of flowers. When her father came home to Italy, he brought beautiful scarves to show her the riches in the New World. They shocked her, burned into her very soul like a sacrament. My mother wanted to shop in the New World; her mother wanted to farm in Italy. It was their lifelong battle.

When Vincenzo was with her in Italy, Michelina could tell that he missed his New World where he worked as a mason, building enormous brick buildings. His skill brought him accolades he never would have heard in Conca, where Michelina's family was so prominent, and where his was so lowly. Michelina was a proud woman, but she knew that a man had pride, too. Her Vincenzo wanted to be proud of his own life, wanted Michelina to be proud of him — even if it meant her giving up everything including her farm, her animals, her sisters, her lifelong friends. It was the one thing he asked of her. Finally she had relented, and packed her bags.

After twenty years of arguing, the family had finally decided: they crossed the ocean to the New World, to Vincenzo's great joy, to Michelina's deepest sorrow. But the family travelled together, all headed in the same direction for the first time in their lives. They could always return to the farm which had been left in the care of the Italian cousins. Michelina held on to that possibility until the day she died. Going home to Italy meant peace; loving the man she married meant no peace ever in this life.

Her sadness never left her. Try as she might she could not forget who she was, and where she belonged. She never belonged in the New World.

My mother stepped off the boat from Italy at age thirteen, and got a job right away in a beauty parlour. She loved it. Cutting hair was not so different from shearing sheep, and the combs, the curls, the waves, even the shampoos were every day a joy to her. She found the dress shops just as her father had promised, full of beautiful things for her to buy. She was used to working hard, she was used to a beautiful world, she enjoyed life, never sad at leaving Italy as Michelina was, angry with Michelina in fact for being so sad.

It was as if the dead twin boys of before her birth were telling my mother to be happy that she was alive, whatever the circumstance, be happy when you're alive. Live life, live, live, live, live, live, as if their foreshortened lives were entrusted to her to live on their behalf.

My mother married my father, the great love of her life, and had five children and three miscarriages. My grandmother, Michelina, lived with us, and so I saw first hand the struggle that went on between them. My grandmother wondered how my mother could be happy here in the New World when she belonged in Italy on the family farm. My mother wondered how my grandmother could be not happy here where life was so lush and delicious. My grandmother wanted to go home; my mother said no. My grandmother wanted my mother to stop bobbing her hair and to stop wearing red lipstick; my mother said no. They argued every day they lived together in my mother's house.

During her life, my mother suffered many serious illnesses, her lungs, her heart, her legs, her hands, not working well and causing episodes of dire concern from her early fifties on. She had gall stones, she had ulcers in her thirties when my father collapsed from overwork and was prescribed rest by his doctor, which meant their young family and their fledgling store were my mother's to manage, at least until my father returned to good health.

Regardless, my mother smiled. In later years, she smiled especially when surrounded by people, such as those she'd been friends with over time, the nuns and priests at the church, the women in the canasta club, her friends in the bridge club, the ladies of the Rosary society who had elected her to the National Council, the Lions Club members who had elected her as their president, she smiled especially when seeing her grandchildren and great-grandchildren, happy with her life even when ill. Always feeling better when she wore her red lipstick, when she had on pretty pajamas instead of a hospital gown, when she could have her hair done every week at the beauty parlour.

If my father had asked her to give up everything she loved in the New World to come with him to Italy to farm, she would have responded exactly as her mother had, stubbornly sure that he had lost his mind, fearful of losing everything that had given her confidence, a sense of purpose, and importance. But in the end, if choosing between life with him or life without him, she would have followed, just as her mother had. Not silently, never silently, but she would have followed.

I watched my grandmother and my mother struggle with each other, getting along and not getting along, always the one wanting the other to be different than they were. I'm certain they never saw that they were at heart the same, merely mirror images of each other, mother and daughter, daughter and mother, one in love with Italy, one in love with the New World, both more in love with their husbands that they could ever admit or express.

Their legacy to me is one of passion. They did not drift aimlessly through life; they engaged life and all its surprises. They may not have had a map, but each had a life to live, and lived it fully, They would expect nothing less of any of their children, expect nothing less of me. It doesn't worry me that my life seems unplanned, or that I seem to have no map to shepherd me.

I live by the guidance of the stars in the night sky: on opposite parts of the heavens my mother and my grandmother shine, arguing as to where I should go, who I should follow, what is my destiny. The sparks between them guide me as all the others who came before me, hot as the fire of Vesuvius flung into the darkened heavens, burning a path of scattered light, shepherding me to where I shall call home.

You Are Here

Letters To My Sons

Salad

Boys, listen to your mother: salad makes you smart. It clears out your gut and that makes you think better. I know that when you're away from home, you get lonely and you eat "comfort" foods; believe me, I understand. There's nothing more comforting than food. But what I do instead is I use a nice hot water bottle. It's just as good as a pet, and almost the same as your father. I'm sending you one to try. It may help you cut down on your comfort foods, you know, cheeseburgers, French fries, noodles with no sauce. It's amazing what we'll eat when we're trying to cope with life. That's why you need to know how to make a good salad. After all is said and done, feeling sorry for ourselves doesn't do us any good. Salad does.

So, to make salad, you need lettuce. I suggest you use Romaine lettuce. It's dark and leafy — and tasty, for lettuce. Just cut off some and tear it into small pieces with your hands. Very earthy. Now wash your cut up lettuce — no soap, just water. Use a strainer. That way the water just goes away, like I wish your Uncle Nick would sometimes, but that's another story. Then put the lettuce in a nice big salad bowl. Now slice up tomatoes on top of the lettuce. Now slice up cucumbers, and put them on top of the lettuce, too. Now add a few pieces of green onion. Your lettuce is looking pretty crowded but that's okay, it's like family. This is your Italian culture. Cherish it.

Next you salt and pepper the tomatoes and cucumbers and then douse them with good strong red wine vinegar. Make sure it's a good Italian red wine vinegar and not one of these vinegars like raspberry or apple-turnover. Now you put some good Italian virgin olive oil over the tomatoes and cucumbers. *Perfetto.* Let your salad sit for at least half an hour so that everything gets to taste like the salad dressing. The salad dressing is the best part of the taste, let's be honest. Then you toss your salad, and eat it.

Stop grumbling and eat it. You can dip some nice crusty Italian bread into the dressing at the bottom, and you'll hear your stomach say "Thanks." You may hear your mother saying thanks, too.

What nice Italian boys I have. Take care,

Love and kisses,

Mom

Adventures In Gardening

It's Springtime, time to plant a garden. I know, you want me to teach you how to cook, not how to garden; but every serious cook knows that fresh grown is the best, and I know you want to be the best because you asked me, not Ronald McDonald, to teach you to cook.

Now, don't get overexcited and plant too much. For just yourself, you'll need only a small patch of garden, because a small patch can grow more than you can imagine. Start small and grow, that's a good rule for life in general, not just gardening. And sit down and think, that's another good rule. You see? Gardening is good practice for life. So you decide what you want to grow in your garden. Not everybody wants the same vegetables in their garden, anymore than everybody wants the same people living in their basement, and you know who I'm talking about. That's life, Mother Nature gives you things and you choose what you want to live with. You learn from your decisions, good and bad. Like Auntie Carmella and her zucchinis, but I won't go into that now.

You plant a few of each of your favorites, a few tomato plants, some peppers, lettuce, some beets, beans and lots of onions. Seed catalogues have pictures that make your mouth water. Some of the produce you buy in the stores tastes like you're eating the picture instead of the real thing, but garden fresh — that's where the real flavour is. When you eat garden fresh you know you're eating something. The whole world suddenly makes sense.

You have to buy your seeds. Then work up your soil so that it's loose — sort of like Uncle Anthony after he's had a few. Then you plant your seeds in rows, marking and labeling the rows so that you know what's what. Knowing what's what is one of life's greatest accomplishments. You'll be so excited watching your garden grow. First the leaves, then the flowers, then the beautiful vegetables — just like raising a family. But don't go getting any ideas, you may be ready for a garden, but that's all for now.

Of course, besides the plants that you want to grow in your garden, weeds will grow as well. Weeds are perfectly nice plants, but if you want to grow a garden, you'll have to restrict it to just your chosen ones. Some people believe God feels the same way about Heaven, but I think God has better things to do than weeding. You, however, are not God, so weed or kiss your garden goodbye. The best way to weed is to keep one step ahead of the weeds — I learned that by being one step behind once too often. But you'll learn your own lessons, just like the rest of us.

Now a word of warning about zucchini. Many people enjoy growing zucchini because zucchini is such a willing grower. It grows more than Baby King Kong in a month. And does it ever produce — it's so fertile, the Pope smiles every time he thinks about zucchini.

Last summer, your grandmother taught me how to cook zucchini blossoms. Yes, even the blossoms are edible. All you do is cut them in half, dredge them in flour, and cook them in olive oil until they're crisp. Terrific, but the growth of the zucchini isn't hampered if you eat the blossoms. *Nothing can stop zucchini*, remember that always. And if you don't pick the zucchini when they're small, they'll grow to be as big and about as tasty as a baseball bat. Auntie Carmella said she was a fool to plant more than one zucchini plant. By the end of summer she felt like she had lived through a horror movie.

Now I don't mean to discourage you, I just want you to be careful. It's a jungle out there. Once you mix the Canadian growing season with the willing and fertile zucchini, you're into more than nice young boys like you can handle. Trust me: you want a nice first experience, stick to the basics. Today peas and carrots, tomorrow melons and zucchini.

For now, I hope you enjoy planning your garden, planting it and watching it grow. Gardening, like life, is a great adventure. Enjoy it, and enjoy the fresh produce, too. And send me pictures. The first fruits are mine, says your mother.

Take care,

Love and kisses,

Mom

Chicken Soup

So when you're away from home with a bad cold, I'm not around to make you chicken soup. I mailed you some, but it's good that I teach you how to make your own too. You can make lots and freeze it, so you're ready to be sick next time. Now, make yourself comfortable, lie back, and I'll tell you all about chicken soup.

Most important is the chicken broth. Without that, who knows what you have. The easiest way to make the chicken broth is to take a whole chicken, a dead one, plucked and cleaned out, yes, yes, yes, but dead for sure. You put your chicken in a big, deep pot, cover it with salted water, and boil it for an hour or so. The water will miraculously turn into chicken broth, as amazing a trick as anyone ever did.

As the chicken is cooking, an awful-looking, brownish-white foam will appear. Stay calm. There's nothing wrong with your chicken. It's just the way they all react to being boiled. Just skim off the foam and act like nothing is wrong. While your chicken is boiling you can try to make yourself feel better by telling yourself a few good chicken jokes, like you used to tell me when you were little. If that doesn't work, take some time to compare yourself to your chicken: You may be sick, but you're better off than your chicken.

Then after your chicken is cooked, take it out of the broth and put it in the fridge for another day's supper. Once you have your chicken broth, all you need to do to make soup is to put some noodles and some vegetables in it. Cook the noodles separately and drain them before you put them in your chicken broth, otherwise, the starch will turn your broth into crazy glue.

For vegetables, I usually put in a little onion, some carrots, celery, maybe a little broccoli. I realize that you hate vegetables, so if you want, cook the vegetables in the broth so that at least you get the vitamins and then take them out. It's a sin, I know, but what can you do? Maybe put them in the freezer and someday you'll appreciate them.

You can either eat your chicken soup now, or if you want, put it in the fridge so that all the fat comes to the top and you can get rid of it. If you ask me, you could use a little extra fat, but it's up to you. This is your soup you've gotten yourself into!

Now dress warm and remember to wear a scarf.

Take care.

Love and kisses.

Mom

How To Cook For A Girlfriend

SOMEDAY MY LITTLE BOYS WILL GROW UP. What can a mother do? Nothing, that's what. So if you want my advice about how to impress your girlfriends, skip the fancy food and give her food from the heart. Show her you care about more than the outside of her body. Show her you care about the inside, too, which I assume you do because you were always such nice boys.

For the appetizer serve fish, because it's brain food. You tell her this, and she'll know you appreciate her mind and want to keep her from going funny in the head. It's not every girl that can say that about her boyfriend.

Just buy a dozen shrimp at the fish market — get the ones already cleaned, because you'll have enough to clean without having to clean shrimp too. Then boil the shrimp just until they turn bright pink. Serve them on a bed of lettuce in a champagne glass, kind of hooked over the edge, like they were sitting up and looking at you. Put a dab of shrimp cocktail sauce and a lemon wedge in the middle of the bed of lettuce. They'll look so pretty, you won't have to give her a corsage.

For your main course, I think you should serve her liver and onions. The liver will build up her blood and she will appreciate that. The onions will keep her from catching a cold, and everyone will appreciate that.

To make the liver, just scramble a raw egg and dip the liver into it, and then dip the liver into some bread crumbs to coat it, so it doesn't get all dried out when you cook it. Did you know the egg kind of acts like a glue, to keep the bread crumbs stuck on? I think that's physics. So, then you sauté the liver in some butter. (Sauté means fry, it's French, you know.) The liver is done when it's not so shaky any more, and when it doesn't bleed. I always cook it extra. You never know what this animal has been into. Better to be on the safe side.

For the onions, you just fry them in some butter and serve them on the liver. Make sure there's lots, you don't want your date to think you're cheap.

Make baked potatoes so your girl doesn't get fat, and you make sure she eats the skin because that's where all the vitamins are. You can serve some nice broccoli for your vegetable. Now I know you'd rather skip vegetables altogether, but you have to take care of yourself, and your girl, too. Close your eyes when you're eating your broccoli; that may help you get it down easier, and she'll think you're being romantic!

For dessert, have something simple. Nothing too sweet, because you want her teeth to stay in good shape. I would suggest some nice fresh fruit to keep her regular. Some apples or pears. Grapes are nice, but they're passion fruit, so maybe not grapes.

If you're stuck for something to say, talk about what a nice family you have, so that she knows you're a nice boy. And you be a gentleman and do the dishes. Don't let your guest do the work just because she's a girl. That's the kind of consideration she'll remember years from now.

And one more thing. Remember, she's coming for supper, not breakfast, eh? Be good.

Love and kisses,

Mom

Aunt Josie

Aunt Josie says to say hello.

You know, if you really want to learn how to cook, it's your Aunt Josie you should be asking, she's the best. Of course, now that she's in Heaven, I guess she's cooking there, not here. But you pray to Aunt Josie, ask her to guide you in the kitchen. She can do that and cook for the angels at the same time.

I've made some of the dishes she used to serve, ones you like so much, like lemon chicken. Lemon chicken is easy to make: you broil the chicken, then five minutes before it's done, you baste it with lemon and olive oil. So simple, but oh, there isn't a faster way to Heaven I know.

I can remember once asking Aunt Josie for the recipe. She looked at me as if I had two heads. "Recipe?" she said. I don't think she ever heard of such a thing before.

She said, "You broil the chicken."

"How long?" I asked.

"Till it's done," she said. "And then you take a little olive oil with a little salt and pepper and lemon juice in it and you put it on the chicken and cook it for a few more minutes."

I remember this olive oil and lemon juice sitting in a cup on Aunt Josie's kitchen counter with a leafy piece of celery sticking out of it. It would be there for hours while Aunt Josie was preparing a meal. Aunt Josie would make the salad, have a little wine, then she'd start the macaroni water, have a little wine, stir the tomato sauce, have a little ... you know, Aunt Josie had a pretty good time in her kitchen. But all the while she'd be cooking, this celery would be sitting in the oil and lemon juice. I asked her what the celery was for, and she said that's how you put the olive oil on the chicken, you use the celery as a brush.

I've made Aunt Josie's lemon chicken lots of times, never as good as Aunt Josie, of course, but some times it's been better than others, and you know what has made the difference? That leafy piece of celery sitting in the oil. A little seemingly insignificant ingredient, but so powerful. Not just because of its flavour, but because it draws the best out of the cook — love, patience, and care. Those ingredients give cooking something very special. You have to remember to put the love in. That's the secret ingredient to good cooking.

So when you said you wanted to learn to cook, did you know you were telling me you wanted to learn about Life and Happiness and Love?

Look at your Aunt Josie. There she was all bent up like a pretzel, weighing hardly more than a girl. She had a hard time talking, eating, everything. But Aunt Josie always had a smile ready. The Senior's Home even asked her to be on their board because she was so wise about life.

When I think of her, I have so many fond memories, and such an admiration for her. I always wonder if she learned to cook so well because she knew how to live well, or if she learned to live well because she cooked well.

So you keep chopping those onions and stirring with care. Someday you may be as happy and content as your Aunt Josie.

Bye for now,

Love and kisses,

Mom

Your Italian Relatives

GRANDMA MICHELINA MARRIED VINCENZO SIMEONE. Her maiden name was Pietrantonio. The Pietrantonio's were the family most prominent in the village of Conca because they had a little land and could grow things. The Simeone's were the least prominent, with no land, no nothing. Your Grandfather Simeone and his family lived in a cave in the mountainside just below Conca.

Grandpa Caruso's father's village was Savingano, his mother's was Grece. All the family villages were situated on mountaintops south of Naples, stone houses, stone stairways, stone streets, carved out of the mountain itself. With so many mountains in their past, Grandma and Grandpa Caruso were always happy to go climbing, up mountainsides, up staircases; they found it invigorating.

The Savingano Caruso's we visited in 1989 have red hair, raise chickens, and grow a garden. They gave us a cheese when we left after our visit.

Your great-great aunt, sister to Michelina, married a Pelligrino, and was the first of our relatives to leave Italy. Who knows what they were thinking.

Grandma Caruso remembers the watermelon festival on the farm in Conca, where the prize went to the reddest and sweetest — not the biggest — watermelon. The farm in Conca grew figs, red cherries, white cherries, walnuts, hazelnuts, olives for olive oil, wheat, corn. There were seven or eight sheep and one goat. There was a horse, too.

When Grandpa Simeone would return to Italy from the New World where he worked as a stone mason, he would stand around and look at all the farming activities. He would listen to the music playing while the corn was gathered. His mind couldn't help itself, it wandered back to the New World. He was not a farmer; he was a builder.

"Uncle Nick" names three of your relatives: Nick Caruso (Grandpa's brother); Nick Capozzoli (Aunt Josie's husband, the tailor, whose son, Louie, wore baloney curls); Nick Ribis (Sicilian, the name shortened from Ribisi, Aunt Angie's husband). Aunt Angie is Grandma's younger sister. Their children are Phyllis, Nicholas, and Michelle. Uncle Alberto was Grandma's older brother who worked all his life in the hat box factory. His wife was Aunt Christina, their children were Vincenzo who married Millie, Adella who married John (who died very young, leaving Adella a young widow alone), and Anthony, the youngest, who never married.

Uncle Nick Caruso and his wonderful wife, Betty, sadly had no children. Louie Caruso and his wife, Bernice, had Donald and Brenda, and the twins (who Grandma thinks were adopted).

Back in the Old Country, Cousin Alberto ran the farm, along with his mother, Olivia. If you go to Italy, look in the graveyards for these names:

Simeone
Pietrantonio
Pelligrino
Capozzoli
Ribisi
Caruso

These are your relatives. Say a prayer when you visit them or their villages, and make a donation to the local church. When you pray to them, ask for assistance in living your life, because they're family, they have to help whether they like you or not. And ask God to forgive your ancestors. They were all good people, but everybody needs forgiveness.

Obituary

ONCE I DIE, YOU'LL ALL COME VISIT ME — dead ones, live ones, you'll gather around, sons, parents, sisters, brother, aunts, uncles, grandmas and grandpas, priests, Daisy my dog, Tuxedo my cat, the Purple Martins who come year after year to the house next door, everybody I ever knew will come see me when I'm dead because, well, that's life. The dead get visitors.

My father's figs and roses, Aunt Josie's ravioli, Grandpa's tomatoes, lettuce, and scallions, Grandma's lullaby, the mulberry tree, the cherry tree, the olive grove in Italy, a box of photographs, a herd of sheep across the ocean, all will come to me when I die. Herds of cows from the pastures along the highway, huge white bulls with majestic heads, angels and archangels, northern lights, stars. Sun dogs and rainbows; and clouds which continually reconfigured themselves into ships and dinosaurs, into old, old men, into geese. The lace-trimmed handkerchiefs Grandma Caruso made, Grandpa Caruso's homemade wine. Prairie grasses and farmers' fields: alfalfa in flower and mustard in bloom. And music, single notes hovering like birds; symphonies, bluebirds singing; owls, coyotes, and whales; operatic tenors, drums and the breathing of the wind. Paintings, sculptures, my house with the verandah, and the one over the store, swings on playgrounds, mirrors and stained glass windows. Two very fine sons full of mystery and surprises and the most tender love. Mom and dad, sisters and a brother, aunts who could cook and clean, and uncles who could laugh. The ancient ones and the spirits of the dead, some with no title except for love. All in all, it will end on a festive and happy note. Life goes on and on and on and the brilliant green grass will wrap around me and carry me home home home home home home home, grateful for a good life.

DONNA CARUSO has worked in a variety of arts disciplines since 1980. She has received many awards for her documentary film and video productions, and for screenwriting. Her book of short fiction, *Under Her Skin* was shortlisted for a Saskatchewan Book Award. Caruso lives in Fort Qu'Appelle, Saskatchewan.